FOR

WHEN

NOBODY

WAS

WATCHING

"The point of the memoir . . . is to show how dedication and a relentless work ethic can overcome an endless series of obstacles, both personal and professional." — *Los Angeles Times*

"*When Nobody Was Watching* provides a harrowing account of athletes' sacrifices. Lloyd's single-mindedness has undoubtedly put her in a different plane to most people." — *Guardian*

"If you are a real soccer player — then this is the book for you to read . . . Open and refreshing . . . From the preface to the epilogue, this book is filled with passion and the solid wisdom of a winner . . . Inspiring and uplifting. Definitely a GREAT READ." — *GoalNation*

"Hard to put down . . . A must-read for women's soccer followers and hopefully [it] sets a standard for future books on the women's game." — *Tribal Football*

"A remarkable portrait of the relentless drive and sacrifice required to truly be the best." — *Booklist*

WHEN
NOBODY
WAS
WATCHING

My Hard-Fought Journey
to the Top of the Soccer World

CARLI LLOYD

with Wayne Coffey

Mariner Books
Houghton Mifflin Harcourt
BOSTON   NEW YORK

First Mariner Books edition 2017

Copyright © 2016 by Carlilloyd.com LLC

www.hmhco.com

Library of Congress Cataloging-in-Publication Data
Names: Lloyd, Carli, date, author. | Coffey, Wayne R., collaborator.
Title: When nobody was watching : my hard-fought journey to the top
of the soccer world / Carli Lloyd, with Wayne Coffey.
Description: Boston : Houghton Mifflin Harcourt, 2016. | Includes index.
Identifiers: LCCN 2016036411 (print) | LCCN 2016039930 (ebook) |
ISBN 9780544814622 (hardcover) | ISBN 9780544976801 (hardcover signed
edition) | ISBN 9780544814554 (ebook) | ISBN 9781328745620 (paperback)
Subjects: LCSH: Lloyd, Carli, date | Women soccer players — United States —
Biography. | Soccer — United States — History.
Classification: LCC GV942.7.L59 L56 2016 (print) | LCC GV942.7.L59 (ebook) |
DDC 796.334092 [B] — dc23
LC record available at https://lccn.loc.gov/2016036411

Book design by Chrissy Kurpeski

Printed in the United States of America
22 23 24 25 26 LSB 9 8 7 6 5

To Brian, my love and husband,
and James, my trainer, friend, and mentor

Contents

Author's Note

This is the story of my soccer journey. It has had many stops along the way, and enough ups and downs to make a miniseries. I've recounted my experiences as faithfully and accurately as possible, but I want readers to understand that, in retracing events that go back decades, some of the quotes, while completely true in spirit and context, may not be word for word as originally stated.

— Carli Lloyd
Mount Laurel, New Jersey
April 2016

Prologue
What You See Is What You Get

I DON'T DO FAKE. That's the first thing you should know about me. I'm not one to put on airs or change my demeanor, depending on where I am or who I am talking to. I don't much care about the red carpet or being on the cover of magazines. I don't put on makeup when I'm getting ready for a game, because why would I? I am gearing up for battle.

How is mascara or eyeliner going to help me win the battle?

If I'm not happy, you can see it on my face from the other end of the Jersey Turnpike. I don't hide it in my body language very well either. My normal way of walking is a borderline strut, shoulders back with a bit of a swaggering defiance in my step, as if I were the new sheriff in town.

If I'm ticked off about something, or you cross me, the strut gets that much more pronounced. I'm as easy to read as the top line of an eye chart.

You hear a lot these days about brand-building and image-crafting. I have a brand. You know what it is? Soccer player. It's the only brand I have any interest in. Of course, I want to be recognized for being a world-class player, but when I wake up every day it's not my goal to figure out how to become a bigger celebrity or have more Twitter followers. If that happens because of what I am doing on the field, great.

Otherwise, I have zero interest.

I've been approached by *ESPN: The Magazine* to pose in the body issue. *Dancing with the Stars* has reached out to me, and so has *Maxim* magazine, for a photo shoot that I'm pretty sure would've had much more to do with skin than soccer. Thanks, but no thanks. A number of prominent athletes — soccer players among them — have been featured in the *Sports Illustrated* swimsuit issue and other publications. It is not a decision that I am judging in any way. To each her own. I'm sure they feel proud of their bodies and see no reason not to show them off. It's just not for me. I want to be a role model, not a runway model. I want to be known for the body of work of my career. If that makes me old-fashioned or out of step with the times we live in, so be it.

I'm always going to be true to how I feel.

Another thing I have no interest in is drama. To me, it is a massive waste of time and energy, siphoning off your fuel and your focus. It's a lesson I've learned, along with a million or so others, from James Galanis, my longtime trainer and mentor, an Australian transplant in South Jersey who has had a greater impact on my soccer journey than anyone. Unfortunately, in a dozen years on the U.S. Women's National Team, I've been around enough drama queens to fill a royal palace. I've seen new players get frozen out by veterans (I was one of the rookies once, and it wasn't fun), and I have seen coaches forced out. I've witnessed drama involving lineup changes and strategic formations, heard gossip about alleged favoritism. There were times when I wondered if I was in a reality TV series. I'm not kidding, and never more so than at the 2007 World Cup, when Hope Solo, my best friend on the team, spoke her mind and certain team leaders did everything but banish her from the human race. Drama doesn't necessarily make anybody a bad person. It's just the way it is. When you have a bunch of high-achieving, uber-competitive, strong-willed women in close quarters, stuff is going to happen sometimes. And it does.

I just don't want to get sucked into it.

Steer clear of anything that isn't helping you get where you want to go — that is another James Galanis lesson, one that has pretty much become my life mantra. If something isn't helping you, it means it's hurting you, and the bigger the goals you have, the less you can afford to have anything impede your progress. This may sound trite, but it's nothing but the truth: all I want to do is work hard and get better and do everything I can to help my team win. That's the sum total of my agenda.

Everything else is chatter.

I have a pretty good idea where my aversion to drama comes from. I've had my fill of it, for a long time, in my own family — my parents and my younger brother and sister. My father threw me out of the house in 2008 in a fit of anger, and I have been on my own island ever since, with only sporadic contact, usually via email or phone calls. When I was honored as the World Player of the Year in January 2016 at a gala in Zurich, Switzerland, I never heard from my parents. When I had arguably the greatest final-game performance in the annals of the Women's World Cup last summer in Canada, I was able to share the joy with Brian Hollins, my fiancé, and my aunts and uncles and cousins and friends, and James of course.

I did not share it with my own parents.

When my father had open-heart surgery, nobody told me until well afterwards. When my sister got married, I was not invited. I love my family and would like nothing more than to reconcile with them. Nobody has done more for me in my life than my parents, who devoted untold amounts of time and money over many, many years that allowed me to play the game I love. It's no exaggeration to say that I never would've gotten anywhere near a World Cup, an Olympics, or the U.S. Women's National Team without them. I have never forgotten that, and I never will.

The fact is that my parents were too devoted — and did too much for me.

Everything they did was well-meaning, but there comes a time when you need to let your kids make their own decisions and get a taste of failure. As I reached my early twenties I started to feel smothered by their attention. They would pepper me with questions about how things were going with the national team and make suggestions about everything from how I should play to how I should conduct myself. Again, it was all out of a desire to help, but it wasn't necessarily what I wanted to hear.

Our differences escalated over time, and as with every family rift, there was plenty of blame to spread around. I am not going to lie. There were times when I was out of line. I absolutely can be stubborn, and I definitely said things I shouldn't have said. I totally own that.

From my perspective, the message I got from my parents, time and again, was that I was doing things all wrong, that they were the victims, and that I needed to listen to them or my career was going to get completely derailed. I believe they wanted the best for me, but somehow, almost every time I talked to them, I felt as if I'd been chopped into small pieces. So I pushed back, and sometimes I pushed back hard. We had a lot of blowups.

Sometimes my parents would write emails or cards and I would answer, but every time we tried to work through it things would blow up again.

It hasn't been easy going it alone. I am sure it hasn't been easy for my parents either. I don't take any joy in writing about strains in our family relationships, but the truth is that it has weighed on me for years now and it has been very much a part of my journey. To become the soccer player I am, I had to grow up, become my own person, and make my own decisions about what to do on the field and in life. Those decisions haven't always been popular with my family, but they were what was right for me. At some point I came to realize that I was no longer the little girl playing for the Delran Dynamite in our neighborhood park, a kid whose parents would bandage her up and drive her all over the place and make sure she had everything she needed. On the field it's just me and the ball and the net, and I knew deep down I had to figure this out for myself. I'm so grateful for all the things my family has done for me along the way, and I wish we could have shared every triumph — and every tear too. James likes to say, "Strength is measured by how far you are willing to push your weaknesses." I want to be strong, work on my weaknesses. I want to believe there's a way to work through this, and that this journey I'm on will include my parents again. I refuse to give up hope.

Near the end of my junior year at Rutgers University in 2003, I got cut from the U.S. U-21 team and decided it was time to quit competitive soccer. I was a college All-American and had accomplished some things, made some national teams, but my dream was to make the full national team, and if I couldn't make the U-21s, how was I going to make the full team? The coach who cut me told me straight out that I wasn't at a national-team level. He said I didn't defend well enough and didn't work hard enough. The coach's name was Chris Petrucelli. He had a brush cut and a square jaw, and I hated him in that moment, hated how he'd squashed my dream as if it were a cockroach on a countertop.

Now?

Now, when I run into Chris Petrucelli, I tell him he's the guy whose honesty played a key role in saving my career.

For more than a decade with the U.S. Women's National Team, I've taken the soccer field feeling as though I have to prove people wrong, starting with Chris Petrucelli. I've often felt overlooked and underappreciated, and at times completely misunderstood. I didn't come out of the University of North Carolina or one of the other popular feeder schools. I was never among the chosen ones when U.S. Soccer coaches talked about the next generation of impact players. Within a few months of scoring the gold medal–winning goal in the Beijing Olympics in 2008, I was told that my contract wasn't being renewed and I needed to play my way back onto the team.

Four years later, I was a fixture at attacking mid and had been named MVP of the CONCACAF Olympic qualifying tournament. Then I was benched by Pia Sundhage after a lackluster showing in our send-off game before going to London. When I scored both goals in the final to carry the U.S. to another Olympic gold, it wasn't just the sweetest possible vindication for me: it was fresh proof that I am one of those athletes who thrives on slights, whether real or imagined. My trainer James calls it "the underdog mentality." He does everything he can to cultivate it, and he's gotten an unintended boost from U.S. Soccer's marketing department, which for years basically ignored me in its promotional initiatives. Before the 2015 World Cup, you might've been able to find a Carli Lloyd U.S. Soccer jersey, but only if you looked hard. Did I lose sleep over that? I did not. Did it annoy me? It did. James knew that and used it, just as he uses it when a writer rips me or I am getting blown up on social media. He knows I am at my best when I am playing with an edge, with some Jersey girl attitude, getting after it like a kid who has had her lunch money stolen and is hell-bent on getting it back.

Neither James nor I have to look far to find doubters and doomsayers about me after the first three games of the 2015 Women's World Cup in Canada. I come into it fitter and more ready than for any tournament I've ever played. It is my third World Cup. In the first one, in 2007, we were demolished by Brazil, 4–0, in the semifinals. In the second, in 2011, we lost to Japan on penalty kicks in the final. I am one of those who missed her PK. I still feel horrible about it.

Now it is time to change the narrative. I am a stronger, better, and mentally tougher player than I have ever been. Never mind that eleven days after the World Cup ends I will turn thirty-three. I am so much better than I was at twenty-three, there's nothing to even talk about. I am ready to crush it, and I believe that we, collectively, have the character and heart and skill to be the first U.S. team to bring home the Cup since 1999.

Then the tournament starts, and after three games we look more like total imposters than the number-two-ranked team in the world. We limp out of Group D with two victories and a tie, advancing mostly because Hope plays out of her mind and Megan Rapinoe scores twice in our opener against Australia, and because our shortest player, Meghan Klingenberg, all five feet, two inches of her, channels her inner pogo stick and heads away what appears to be a certain goal for Sweden in our second game. We're not possessing the ball much, and we're creating even less, and what little attacking we are doing seems to completely bypass the center midfielders, Lauren Holiday and me. My confidence — soaring at the start — goes into the Dumpster faster than you can say Sepp Blatter. I feel uninvolved, ineffective, and oddly lethargic. I take pride in my ability to impact a game from one box to another, making tackles and rebuffing an opponent's attack on one end, and taking on defenders 1 v. 1 or threading a through pass or letting fly with a blast on the other end. Except for short stretches here and there, I feel as though I am doing almost none of that through the first 270 minutes of the 2015 Women's World Cup.

The good news is that we are heading into the elimination round, regardless of our patchy performances. The bad news for me is that my confidence is at an all-time low. I room with Hope for the first two games in Winnipeg, and when we check in there are action posters of ourselves on our beds, placed there by Dawn Scott, our fitness trainer, and other team staffers and personalized with three words.

Mine are:

Committed. Relentless. Confident.

If you are scoring at home (and I am), I'm 0-for-3, batting zero, and disgusted with myself.

I am a bit of a strange mix in the self-belief department. I have an almost unshakable faith in my ability to come through when it matters most and to prevail no matter what the odds. But that faith exists side by side with a stubborn, lifelong penchant for demanding perfection of myself and for beating up on myself when I fall short of it. The result is that it is dangerously easy for me to hold on to mistakes, keeping them alive in an endless loop of self-criticism.

Some people can just shrug off a bad game. I've heard baseball experts say that the reason Mariano Rivera was the greatest closer in history was because he had the greatest gift an athlete can have: a short memory. Whenever he made a mistake, giving up a hit or blowing a save, he'd forget about it instantly and get back on the mound and put everything into the next pitch. He lived his whole competitive life in the moment, which of course is exactly where you want to be.

The trouble for me isn't only the expectations I have for myself, but also my tendency to be super-responsible. I take things seriously. I don't want to let anybody down. Not Brian or James, or my family and friends, or my fans. When I believe I haven't played up to my standards, it's as if I'm walking around with a ball and chain.

Jill Ellis meets with me before we take on Colombia in our first knockout game, in Edmonton.

"I know you are frustrated," Jill says. "But don't worry. We are going to get you going. We know what you are capable of. We know your history of coming through when the stakes are the greatest. Don't take on any huge responsibility. Don't force things. Just let it happen. You play your game, and you will be fine."

At the depth of my despondence, I do what I always do in times of doubt or crisis. I reach out to James Galanis. He's on a Greek island with his family, on vacation.

"You didn't turn into a bad soccer player overnight," James says. "That is not possible. If you guys as a team were attacking and scoring goals, this wouldn't be an issue and nobody would be talking about what a disappointment the U.S. has been."

James underscores the same point Jill made: *Don't come out of the box in the next game and try to be perfect and change everything all at once. Don't be too fancy. Don't go for magic right out of the chute. Just go out and have fun and play. Build up slowly. Play simple balls. Connect on some passes. Get some confidence on the ball. Let yourself ease into the game, and before you know it you will be back to being Carli.*

James has one more piece of wisdom.

"When this World Cup is over, nobody is going to be talking about what happened in the group stage," he says. "They're going to be talking about the player and players who are the strongest and fittest and are powering through when everybody else is hitting their wall. They'll be talking about the players who refuse to let their team lose.

"They will be talking about you, Ms. Lloyd."

I want to believe him. I do believe him.

I get off the phone and think about how I've gotten through every other disappointment and challenge in my career: By going back to work. By working when nobody is watching, and then working some more. *You don't back off. You don't pay attention to negativity in your head. You refuse to give in.* That is what's going to set me free and get me fully engaged in this tournament.

There are, potentially, four single-elimination games left in our World Cup. I replace the loop of self-criticism in my head with something different:

It is not how you start that matters, it's how you finish.

I walk through the tunnel in Commonwealth Stadium before we take on Colombia in the round-of-sixteen, holding hands with a little kid in a bright yellow shirt and red shorts. My World Cup starts now. I am ready. You can see it plainly on my face, because I don't do fake.

1

Beginnings

FOURTEEN MILES EAST OF THE LIBERTY BELL, the small, blue-collar community of Delran, New Jersey, stretches along U.S. Route 130, a busy run of road with an abundance of diners, car lots, and chain restaurants, long on neon and short on charm. Its name comes from the first three letters of DEL-aware River and RAN-cocas Creek, both of which flow through the area on their way to Delaware Bay. If you want a quaint, moneyed town, there are a number of them to choose from in the area, but keep on driving because that is not Delran. My family has a modest neighborhood colonial that sits diagonally, on the corner of Black Baron Drive and Parry Road, offering a side yard that is big enough to practice free kicks. There is a curb out front and two parks just down the street, and I don't need a whole lot more.

From as early as I can remember, I am a kid in motion. I want to be active and to play sports, and I definitely do not mind taking risks. The kitchen counter isn't just a place for my mother to prepare her flank steak or meat loaf — it's a climbing platform. One time I scramble onto it and stand up, just to take in the view. I somehow get my eyelid caught on a cabinet door. Not an easy feat to pull off, but I do it. I slice up my eyelid enough that we have to go to the emergency room to get stitches. My eyelids have not gone near a cabinet door since.

I keep pushing limits. In first or second grade, I take swimming lessons at the YMCA in nearby Moorestown. I'm not sure what stroke we are working on at the time, but during one lesson I get in over my head and drop below the surface. My mother sees my head disappear and springs out of the bleachers and dives in to get me. She is in street clothes, and she makes a quality save. I keep up with the lessons and get to be a good swimmer. I join a team and love competing in the meets, but diving into a cold pool first thing in the morning for training isn't really my thing. I decide the chlorinated world isn't for me.

Just about every other sport, though, I am all over. The Philadelphia sports teams are just across the Delaware River, and I root for all of them. I love the Phillies' slugging catcher, Darren Daulton, and want to wear number 10 because that's the number he wears. I love Lenny Dykstra's grit, and the edgy brilliance of the Sixers' Allen Iverson, and the punishing power of the Flyers' Eric Lindros. I don't see the world through a prism of gender. I have zero interest in being a girlie girl. I don't have a Barbie collection; I have baseball cards and Matchbox cars. As soon as my parents think I am old enough I become our lawn-care person. I love mowing the lawn because I want to be like my father. I hate it when my parents make me wear a dress or skirt to church or school. I want to wear sports clothes, clothing that will allow me to play in case a game breaks out someplace. For my school picture in fifth grade at Millbridge Elementary, I wear blue-and-purple overalls, with a blue-and-purple shark watch and my black-and-blue indoor soccer shoes. You will never find a ribbon or bow on me.

Nor do I have one on the day I get in some big trouble at Millbridge. During recess a bunch of boys are heaving rocks across a blacktop parking lot at the back of the school grounds, aiming for a tree line on the other side. On the other side of the tree line are some houses. I am a shortstop. I can make the throw to first from deep in the hole, and I figure I have as good an arm as the rest of them, so I join in, firing a few rocks of my own. It isn't the best idea, since airborne rocks on playgrounds rarely lead to anything good. I clear the blacktop easily with my tosses, an accomplishment that earns me my first and only trip to the principal's office.

Otherwise, I do a good job of staying out of trouble and not getting caught by the authorities. Mrs. Goodwin is one of my favorite teachers, and it's good that I like her so much because I have her six different times in middle and high school. In American Literature class in eleventh grade, she turns away for a moment and something possesses me to throw a Nerd from the back of the class. The Nerd hits her in the shoulder. She's the nicest person, but now she is ticked off, and you can't blame her.

"Who threw that?" she demands to know.

I am terrified, already ridden with guilt. I do not cop to it; I am too afraid of the consequences. I don't fully expunge my guilt until years later.

"Remember when you got hit by the Nerd, Mrs. Goodwin?" I say. "That was me. I am sorry." She laughs and accepts my confession.

In high school, late one night, a bunch of friends pile into my car — actually my mother's car, a Chrysler Town and Country minivan — and take a spin around the school track. We're laughing all the way around and then go back to regulation roads with no Delran police cars in sight. That is it for my wild life of crime.

Willfulness, however, has been a part of my makeup for a long time. I pick my battles and fight them with vigor. When my parents say no, it isn't the end of the conversation — it's the start of a debate. I love Fruity Pebbles and Fruit Rollups as a kid, but I am a seriously picky eater otherwise. I become very adept at the scoop-and-sneak technique. If my mother serves me food that isn't acceptable, I wrap up the offending items — asparagus, beets, and my mother's meat loaf are at the top of the list — into a napkin, excuse myself, and then go to the bathroom, where I flush the evidence down the toilet. (I am a very healthy eater these days and am appalled at much of what I did as a kid, but isn't that what growing up is supposed to be about?)

My parents, Steve and Pam Lloyd, work hard to provide for my brother, my sister, and me. Dad manages his machine shop, and Mom is a paralegal secretary. We are a long way from wealthy, but we have everything we need, and, limited means or not, my parents do everything they can to support all of us, especially my soccer. I play basketball and softball too, but from the time I start kicking a soccer ball at age five it is my favorite thing to do. One of the greatest thrills of my whole childhood is when my parents buy me my first pair of Copa soccer shoes. I am nine years old, and when I put them on for the first time I don't feel like a kid imposter anymore. I feel legit. They are black leather, and they are my pride and joy. I clean them after every game and practice, meticulously applying leather conditioner. I want them to stay new-looking. I want them to last forever.

I am that way with all my stuff. My room is purple, my favorite color, and always tidy. I dust the shelves and my trophies and plaques and make my bed, and I can't stand having stuff strewn around on the floor. I keep my money in my piggybank and always know how much is in there. I keep careful track of my special blanket and my teddy bear. I lay out my clothes the night before school, and my uniform the night before games, with my autographed photo of former U.S. men's team player Cobi Jones and a poster of Ronaldinho as my inspiration. By the time I am in eighth grade I am doing all my own laundry because I want to make sure my uniform is just so.

I don't *like* order. I love order.

I am like that in all areas of my life. I am the queen of to-do lists. At my desk in school, the pencils are sharpened and lined up, the notebooks and textbooks and handouts neatly stacked. My soccer bag isn't a jumble of water bottles and pre-wrap and stinky old shin guards. It is clean and well organized, everything in its place, no fishing expeditions required. I have no idea that being a professional soccer player will ever be a career option — I think it would be cool to be an FBI agent — but even as a little girl I take soccer seriously. Nobody ever has to tell me to practice because it is all I want to do.

The first team I play on is the Delran Dynamite. I am tiny and fast and play up front. Teaming up with my friends Kim and Michelle, we may not quite be dynamite, but we are pretty good. Michelle's mom, Karen Thornton, is the coach, and my dad is the assistant coach. Mrs. Thornton does most of the talking and motivating. My dad is on the quiet side, which I appreciate, because you run across so many coaches who scream at referees and their players and act like complete jackasses. He likes to set up his chair by the corner flag. My dad is always there, and it is great that he is.

Mrs. Thornton is an experienced coach who has been around sports her whole life. She teaches us and motivates us and exhorts us to have fun; she is positive without being smothering.

"Carli internalized everything," Mrs. Thornton says years later. "I only had to say something once and then she went out and did it. She was the first one at practice every time, with the ball under her arm, ready to go. She was never one of those kids who sang songs on the bench. She was there to play and play her best."

During one Dynamite game, we fall behind in the first half, and at halftime Mrs. Thornton pumps us up with her best Herb Brooks–type, "this moment is yours" speech. We are still behind with five minutes to play, trying our best in our gold-and-white uniforms, but not breaking through when Mrs. Thornton ramps up the urgency.

"Somebody's got to get one!" Mrs. Thornton says. Kim, our goalkeeper, makes a stop and rolls the ball out. I come back and get it. I dribble past one opponent, then another. I pass midfield and get into some open space, then elude another defender. Nearing the box, I beat the last defender who has a chance to stop me and bang a shot past the goalkeeper. On the sideline, Mrs. Thornton throws up her arms and shouts her delight. I am eleven years old at the time, and beyond ecstatic, not merely because I've scored a goal but because all the time and effort I've put into practice has paid off, a tangible reward for a thrill that will never get old.

I don't need a team or even a field to practice. How many times as a kid do I head out to Black Baron Drive with my soccer ball and tap the ball against the curb? A thousand? Ten thousand? I don't know. I just know it's a whole lot. I hit the ball again and again, trying hard to keep control even as it caroms back hard off the concrete. The cracks in the curb are my goalposts. I shoot righty. I shoot lefty. The asphalt isn't good for the cover of my ball. The repetition is very good for my ball skills.

When I need competition, my ball and I make the short trek through the neighborhood to Vermes Field, named for Peter Vermes, a former member of the U.S. Men's National Team who is from Delran, or Don Deutsch Soccer Complex, named for a man who did as much as anyone to promote and grow youth soccer in Delran. I find lots of soccer balls that people have kicked into the woods and don't mind scavenging for them. The more soccer balls I have, the more of them I can kick. There are always boys and men from the neighborhood playing at the fields. Many of them are Turkish. I hop in and play with them all the time. I love playing free soccer. I learn to solve problems on the field, figure things out, get comfortable with the ball on my foot against good competition.

I don't know it at the time, but this is the best thing I ever could've done for my development as a soccer player. There is so much to be gained from playing this sort of soccer, unconstrained by constant whistles and overzealous coaches hollering to do this and or do that. A good coach is indispensable, but for me the best way to learn is to be in the laboratory on my own, free to create and experiment, finding different ways to beat somebody off the dribble or tighten up my touches. Soccer has come a long way in the United States, but I believe our young players are overcoached, from too young an age. There is too much organization and not enough intuition and creativity. The more we encourage kids to just go out and play pickup games, the more they will love it and the faster they will improve.

Competition, and wanting to get better, is what drives me, so I make the difficult decision to leave the Dynamite, a town team, for a nearby club team. Soccer starts to take over my life, in a good way. My role model is my first cousin, Jaime Bula, who is a star soccer, basketball, and softball player who gets a college scholarship. Jaime is five years older than me. I don't have an older sister, but I don't need one with Jaime in the family. She is who I want to be in life. I think, *If I can ever be as good an athlete as Jaime, that would be a dream come true.* She isn't just a great athlete. She is a great person. Treats everybody the right way. She is as tough as she can be as a competitor, and as nice as she can be when the game is over. In college she suffers a devastating knee injury and grinds through a nine-month rehab process and makes it back for the start of the soccer season. She does it with total heart and perseverance. I am in awe of Jaime's will and drive.

It teaches me a wonderful lesson: there is no substitute for hard work. Talent is great. Who doesn't want to have talent? But it's the people who work the hardest and are committed to do the most with the talents they are given who are going to get places.

I go after things the same way Jaime does, especially in school. I am not the world's greatest student. Other kids often seem to pick things up more quickly, but I do all my work, and do it the best way I know how. The effort produces good grades, even though I remain insecure about myself as a student all the way through. When I take tests, whether multiple-choice or true/false, I tend to doubt my answers, and I agonize over whether I have gotten them right.

Perfection is my goal, and that can work for you and against you. It's great to have high standards, because I don't think you ever get anywhere in life trying to be average or just good. On the other side, you can torment yourself along the way if you have impossibly high expectations. You can make the journey hard and joyless if you never allow yourself a few moments of contentment because you are pushing so hard to do even better. This is the line I walk constantly, and it's thinner than the shoelaces of my Copas.

"Perfectionism is the voice of the oppressor, the enemy of the people," the writer Anne Lamott once said. "It will keep you cramped and insane your whole life."

Even in soccer, as I move up in age and competition levels, there are doubts and insecurities. I make New Jersey's Olympic Development Program (ODP) team, and then the ODP Region I team, made up of the top players from thirteen states.

When I first get to the Region I camp, I size up the other players, especially the midfielders. There is Joanna Lohman, from Silver Spring, Maryland, and Sue Flamini, another Jersey girl from the town of Cranford. They are stud center mids. I watch them play and think, *I will never be at their level.* The next step after Region I is making a U.S. national team. No way I can see that happening with players such as Joanna and Sue around.

Joanna goes on to a stellar career at Penn State, a three-time All-American who makes the U.S. Women's National Team and now plays for the Washington Spirit in the National Women's Soccer League (NWSL). Sue accepts a scholarship to the University of Tennessee and is now a big star as well, making national teams of her own.

In Region I camp, I compare myself to them constantly. I stress about not measuring up to them. I wish that weren't the case, but it is. I worry that I simply won't be good enough and won't keep advancing.

When the U.S. women capture the World Cup in the Rose Bowl in 1999, beating China on penalty kicks, I am totally inspired. I attend one of their games before the final and bring the team poster I have and get the autographs of Kristine Lilly, Joy Fawcett, Julie Foudy, Carla Overbeck, and others. Seeing them reach the summit of the sport ratchets up my dream even more.

Can you imagine what it would be like to play in the Olympics and win a gold medal? Can you imagine what it would be like to win a World Cup?

It's hard to wrap my head around it, but I try. I wonder if I will ever get anywhere near such accomplishments.

You can do it if you keep getting better and work harder than everybody else, one voice inside me says.

You've got no shot. You're not even as good as Joanna Lohman and Sue Flamini, another voice says. *And what about all the other great center mids in all the other regions around the country? Who are you kidding?*

But the first voice insists: *If you work hard and keep believing, you have a chance.*

Why are you deluding yourself? the second voice answers.

Like fencers on a strip, swords raised, the voices keep dueling. I worry about which voice will prevail. I know which one I want to listen to. I am a South Jersey girl, and I love soccer, and I want to keep playing at the highest level I can. I don't know what level that is, but I resolve that I will keep going for it. I am going to channel my inner Jaime and think about all she did to get back from her knee injury. I put a lot into soccer and play all the time, but I know I can do more and work harder. It occurs to me that maybe being insecure is a good thing, because it means that you will never get complacent.

Nobody understands this, or me, more than my boyfriend Brian. Brian is two years younger, but just one grade behind me in school. He lives in the same neighborhood, just a few blocks away from Vermes Field. His best friend lives next door to my aunt Patti, so when I am over there visiting I see him riding his dirt bike or hanging out. We get to be good friends, in an athletic, adolescent way, united by our mutual love of sports. Brian plays on the Delran High boys' soccer team, but his best sport is golf. At the beginning of golf season, I find myself intrigued by the sport and show up at some of the practices and try my hand at it. Brian and I start spending more time together, and I find out from a friend of mine that he likes me. I like him too. It's so easy to be with him. He is kind and thoughtful in a quiet, understated way, the opposite of the sort of guys who are always acting up and drawing attention to themselves. Brian is bravado-free, and it's such a great quality. Our first night out together is a double date at the movies, at the Millside Theater on Route 130 in the heart of a Delran shopping center. I think we go to see a horror movie. I am scared by the movie, and happy to be with Brian.

Right from the start, I can see how devoted Brian is, how he would do anything for me. He is further along on the romantic-feelings front than I am in the beginning, but I catch up fast. If I am not studying or playing soccer, I am pretty much with Brian. His dad has a boat and a few WaveRunners, and we like to go out and zip around on them in Rancocas Creek, and I join his family on camping trips to Raystown Lake in Pennsylvania. In one part of the lake there are three different outcroppings where you can jump off into the water.

The lower one is maybe a ten-foot drop. Next is probably a twenty-foot drop, and the top level must be forty or fifty feet up. It's insanely high. I do not scare easily, and neither does Brian. I have never met a roller coaster I wouldn't go on. The hairier the ride, the more time upside down, the steeper the vertical drop, the better. Brian is the same way. We jump off the top outcropping far over Raystown Lake, feet first. By the time I hit the water, I feel as if I am close to the speed of light.

I love it.

Brian's family has another favorite — and much saner — activity at Raystown Lake. They all like to golf, and they are big hitters. They have this contest in which they tee up the ball on one side of the water and see if they can hit it to the other side, well over 300 yards away. Nobody makes it, but they get close. One time I tell them I want a shot at it. I have just climbed out of the water, in a soaking-wet bikini. I get a club and stand over the ball and am determined to mash it, far over the water, and show them I can compete. I draw the club back and come through the ball with all the power I can muster . . . so much so that the driver flies out of my hands, winging high and far into the lake. The club goes farther than the ball. They all think it's hilarious. I feel terrible about losing the club. It was Brian's cousin's brand-new driver. We all go out into the water and dive down and try to find it, with no luck.

Next time I will towel off before I try to hit a ball over the lake, I tell myself.

The outings with Brian and his family are so nourishing, so much fun. The more I am with him, the more I appreciate the goodness of his heart and the steadiness of his demeanor. I struggle so much with my pursuit of perfection in other parts of my life, with doubts about how I am going to measure up. I don't have to reach any standard when I am with him, don't have to be anything but myself. You hear people talk often about unconditional love, but Brian demonstrates it every minute we are together. Every birthday or special occasion, he fills up almost every inch of the card with his thoughts and feelings.

If we share an appetizer or a dessert, he always insists that I take the last bite. It's a small thing, but it means a lot to me.

Early on in our relationship, I realize how lucky I am to have a guy like Brian to care about me. I think, *He would be a wonderful man to spend my life with.* I've never been more right about anything in my life.

2

Strikers Forever

WHEN I AM TWELVE YEARS OLD, I have what feels like a co-
lossal, crush-my-world setback. It's an own-goal loss in a World Cup
final, a walk-off home run for the other guys in a World Series. I have
done all I can with the Delran Dynamite, and I decide to try out for
the South Jersey Select team, which is *the* destination for all of the
elite players in the area. If you are any kind of player, this is where
you want to be.

If your goal is to play at the highest level, this is where you *need*
to be.

I am a star player for the Dynamite, but even at this age I know
that doesn't mean too much. I need to trade up my local pond for a
bigger body of water. I need to get in with the big fish and see if I can
swim.

I go to the Select tryout, and from the time I get out of my dad's
car the experience is daunting. I see platoons of kids milling around
everywhere, more than I've ever seen at a tryout before. Almost all of
them are much bigger than me. I am used to being one of the smallest kids out there. It's never mattered before, so I try to talk myself
into not being intimidated.

You can play with any of them, I tell myself.

I want to believe that, but do I really know it's true? Isn't that why
I am here — to see how I measure up? Tryouts are a strange phenom-

enon, a nonstop parade of insecurities and doubts. You look this way and that and make snap judgments about people's size, strength, character, and playing ability, all of it pretty much based on nothing. You compare yourself constantly to all of those around you:

Whoa, that girl looks tough.

Geez, that girl looks mean.

And that kid over there, wow, she looks really athletic. You think I can take her 1 v. 1?

When you do something well at a tryout, you instantly look up to see if any of the evaluators have noticed, hoping to catch them writing down your number and nodding to each other. If you do something poorly, you hope they were checking a text message or watching somebody else screw up. It's wickedly competitive, all of us wannabe Select players going for the same blue ribbon, as if we were prize pigs at the county fair, all of us desperately hoping that the evaluators — these strangers with clipboards who suddenly are the most important people in your life — are favorably impressed.

Part of you wishes you could help them along:

Hey, did you see that first touch? That through ball? Can you tell how much it means to me to be on this team?

You want to holler all these things. You want to tell them how you don't just love soccer — you need it the way most other people need oxygen. You wish that you could give them a reading of your desire, but you do not get a private audience. So you just play. You try to be at your absolute best and to make an impression.

You do everything you can to win the blue ribbon and make the team.

The tryout ends. The list is posted. Your name is not on it. The evaluators have had a good look at everyone and have decided you are not Select quality. There is no gray in tryouts. You either make the cut or you don't.

I do not make it.

I am devastated.

It is the first time this has happened in my years of playing soccer. I never want to show the world my emotions, and this time is no exception, but in my room it's a waterworks show beneath the Ronaldinho poster, a maelstrom of hurt and anger and disappointment that won't let up. I keep replaying the tryout in my head, wondering what I could have done differently. It's a pointless exercise, of course. It just flings open the doors to self-torture.

My parents say all the right things.

"You can learn from this and use it to make yourself better," my dad says. "You can turn this negative into a positive."

"This happens to everybody at some point. It isn't the end of the world, even though it might feel like it," my mom says.

I am not able to take in much of the comfort, though. I am not sure how long I beat myself up for not making Select, but it goes on for a while, until I get a letter in the mail. It is from a man named Joe Dadura. He is starting a U-13 team at a club in a nearby town. It's called the Medford Strikers. He says he saw me at the Select tryout and thinks I am a good player. He is reaching out to other players who he believes have potential. New Jersey is a congested little state mostly associated with its Turnpike and its Shore, its straight-talking people and traffic tie-ups, but it's also a place that produces as many good soccer players per capita as any region in the country. Joe Dadura's goal is to find enough of these players and coach them the right way and build a team that can compete with anyone.

Soon I am wearing number 10 in the red, white, and black of the Medford Strikers and traveling three times a week to Lumberton, New Jersey, a township that was once a stop on the Underground Railroad; runaway slaves hid in the bottom of a well at a house on Creek Road.

In no time at all I am completely sold on life as a Striker. I am part of a core of players that includes Joe's daughter, Kacy, Maureen Tohidi, Venice Williams, and Quinn Sellers. They are really good players and even better teammates. We do well right off, and it all starts with Mr. D, as we call him, a kind and warmhearted guy who pushes us hard and is supercompetitive but still creates a nurturing and fun team atmosphere.

Mr. D is not a typical soccer coach in any way. He didn't grow up playing or come up through the coaching ranks; he taught himself the game by reading books, going to clinics, and watching videos. Eager to coach his three daughters, he wanted to learn enough to be able to do it. Mr. D owns a tire business, but as far as I can tell he spends every spare second coaching soccer, with his Medford Strikers hat and jacket his regular uniform.

It doesn't take me long to figure out that the Medford Strikers are the best team I've ever been a part of. From the back line to the front line, there are strong players all over the field. Mr. D's emphasis is on quick ball movement, clean touches, building a possession-centered attack and sound, stout defense in the back. I am in center midfield, still a half-pint, relying on technical skill and quick, darting runs as I probe for defensive weaknesses, knocking the ball wherever it needs to be knocked.

I want to be in the middle of everything, all the time, on the field and off. Maureen says I remind her of a gnat, flitting here and there, finding fresh ways to annoy people, whether it's at practice or on our trips to tournaments, which seem to come up almost every weekend. I jump on people's backs when they don't expect it. I sneak up from behind and try to trip them up. I steal their candy and squeeze my way onto a sofa when there is no room for a regulation-sized person. My teammates start calling me PITA, as in Pain In The Ass. PITA doesn't just become my nickname: it becomes my identity, and even part of my email address.

I am in constant motion, an undersized prankster on the prowl, but on the field I am all business. I am out there to compete and to win, as if little PITA undergoes a personality transplant the moment she crosses the line onto the field. We are in Florida one time for a big holiday tournament, and it's raining hard and the field is a mess. We are wearing all-white uniforms. I get pushed from behind by an opponent — no whistle — and go face first into the mud. When I get to my feet, I am covered in the stuff.

"I would've been furious, but Carli just brushed off as much of the mud as she could and kept playing," Venice says later. "She wasn't a fighter or someone to get in your face, but she was going to get her payback by doing a crazy move and scoring on you, and that's what she did this time. On the next play she beat somebody and scored on a long shot."

Venice is right. I get my revenge where it counts the most. Seeing the opponent have to take the ball out of their net is one of the best feelings on earth.

Mr. D encourages unselfishness and team-oriented play, and it's what I love most about this team. Kacy is a really good player, a midfielder who plays alongside me, but Mr. D doesn't build the team around his daughter or around any one player. We all feel important and valued on the Medford Strikers. There isn't any griping or sniping, and nobody acts as if she is the person who makes the whole thing go. The ball moves, and the glory is spread around. It's a beautiful thing when that happens. And because no petty stuff is going on, we have the best time at practices and tournaments and fun follows us around. In one out-of-state tournament, there's a boys' hockey event going on at the same time and we are sharing a hotel with a bunch of young hockey players. Mr. D has a strict curfew of 10:00 PM before early games, but this time a teammate of mine and I decide to venture out to see where the hockey players are hanging out. It's more mischievous than anything, but when we are not back by the time Mr. D does his bed check, we are toast.

"You're sitting out the first half tomorrow," Mr. D tells me.

I know better than to try to talk him out of it. I never blow curfew again.

Lots of times at the end of practice, I have fun without running afoul of any rules. I go to the center of the field and line up a couple of balls on the midfield line. I look toward the empty goal, about fifty yards away. I take a few steps back, sprint up to the first ball, plant my left foot beside it, and swing my right leg into it as if it were a sledgehammer, pounding it as far as I can. I do the same thing with the remaining balls, then go round them up and do it again. When I hit the ball just right, I can just about reach the goal. It's a great feeling when I do. I wonder what it would be like to try to score from there in a game.

Just as Mr. D had planned, the Medford Strikers emerge as a major player in Jersey soccer. Our core five players — Kacy, Maureen, Quinn, Venice, and me — stay together for six years. We win two consecutive New Jersey State Cup titles and soar into the national rankings. But even as we do I struggle at times with my own expectations. I want every touch to be immaculate, every pass to be on target, every shot to find the back of the net. Of course that doesn't happen, but I am not very good at cutting myself any slack. Mistakes stay with me, gnaw at me. Maureen, our captain, has radar for it and helps snap me out of it. In one game I take a shot from distance, a good ten yards outside the 18, and miss badly. Two more shots follow, both way off target, and then both of my hands go to my head and my head drops.

Those are the telltale signs. Maureen doesn't want to see it, or hear it.

"Forget about it, PITA. Keep plugging away. You'll get the next one," she says.

It's a pointed, on-field intervention, and I need it. Maureen has a great knack for helping me get through the thicket of self-criticism. She knows when I start to lose it almost before I do. I am still learning to deal with adversity and not to let my emotions career out of control, particularly when I am thrust into a new situation.

I make the New Jersey Olympic Development Program team in 1996, at age fourteen, all five feet, one inch, and 105 pounds of me. The way ODP works is that, at the end of the year, all the players in the program from the thirteen states in Region I attend a regional camp at the University of Massachusetts. The camp lasts almost a week, and at the end of it a Region I pool team consisting of the top eighteen players is selected. Every morning during the week a list of the players who have made the pool team for that day is posted. Then a final list is posted on the day the camp closes.

I am a mess of nerves and anxiety the whole week. For one thing I am terribly homesick and call home to talk to my parents all the time, but the bigger issue is that I'm constantly making comparisons. I look around and see this staggering assemblage of soccer talent and convince myself that I am out of my league. That this is not true is irrelevant; it's the tape that is playing in my head, and it isn't doing me any favors. In fact, it holds me back big-time. It's hard to play freely when the gears of your brain never stop churning.

I do not make the final posted list. It's a major blow, but it teaches me an invaluable lesson about confidence. I learn that if you don't approach the game with the right mentality, you have no shot to deliver your best. I learn that, as the saying goes, "to compare is to despair." Gradually—very gradually—I also learn that I am the most free, having the most fun and playing my best, when I am focused completely on my own game, not worrying about what everybody else is doing. I learn this the same way I learn how to execute a side volley or a chest trap: by doing the training, doing the reps, because it is only through rigorous training that you are going to get where you want to go. I keep working at focusing on my own game. It is my solution to every challenge.

3

Smackdown

FOR A GUY WHOSE DAY JOB IS TIRES, Mr. D sure gets a lot of traction out of his Medford Strikers. We become one of the top teams in the country, which gets us into high-profile tournaments, which in turn brings packs of college coaches to our tournament games, with scholarship offers in tow.

Maureen Tohidi is offered a full ride to Syracuse. Quinn Sellers accepts a scholarship from Villanova, and Venice Williams (University of South Carolina–Spartanburg) and Kacy Dadura (Niagara) do the same.

We're not the Phillies or Eagles, but the Medford Strikers become quite a sensation in South Jersey. There are photos and glowing write-ups about us in the *Philadelphia Inquirer,* the *Burlington County Times,* and South Jersey's *Courier-Post.* Soccer fans know about us and our championship pedigree. My father, the unofficial chronicler of our acclaim, carefully cuts out all the clippings he can gather. He always brings them up to my room to make sure I know about them.

"Look what they wrote in the paper," he says. Then he takes the clips down to his desk in the garage, where he spends hours — and I mean dozens of hours over many years — arranging and pasting and painstakingly putting together the most comprehensive scrapbooks you have ever seen. My dad never wants to miss anything, and I don't think he ever has.

I have interest from dozens of colleges, an exciting if overwhelming thing to look forward to after my four years at Delran High School, where our team goes to two state finals and I'm named Burlington County Player of the Year in my junior and senior years. I boil the competition down to two finalists: West Virginia and Rutgers. I really like the West Virginia coach, Nikki Izzo-Brown. She has built a strong program, and talking to her convinces me that she can help make me a better player and catapult me to a higher place on the national radar. That is the whole goal — to get seen by the talent evaluators at U.S. Soccer and make my way onto a national team. (I am named to the U-18 national team in 1999, but since we never have an actual camp or compete against other countries, it feels like a credential on paper only.)

Ultimately, I say no to Coach Izzo-Brown — one of the hardest things I've ever had to do — to stay in New Jersey and go to Rutgers and play for Coach Glenn Crooks.

It couldn't go much better at the start at Rutgers, where I bond instantly with two of my favorite all-time teammates, Christine Wentzler and Tara Froehlich. We live together in a dormitory called Stonier Hall, an unsightly brick box with a splendid location in the heart of campus, and we remain roommates for three years in off-campus housing. Christine, Tara, and I are inseparable — except for when they patronize Rutgers's famous Grease Trucks. These are a string of lunch wagons on College Avenue that serve so-called Fat Sandwiches — sub rolls stuffed with burgers, chicken fingers, French fries, mozzarella sticks, bacon, and more, all thrown in together.

I eat one Fat Sandwich, get sick, and never have another.

The results on the soccer field are far more appetizing. We have a strong season in the Big East and get an at-large bid to the NCAA tournament, only the second in school history. We trounce Boston University in the first round and then upset number twenty-two Princeton in the second, advancing to a round-of-sixteen against perennial heavyweight North Carolina, which is 21-0 and gunning for its customary national championship. Even though we are playing on Carolina's home field, we give the team one of its toughest tests of the season, going up a goal in the first half before losing 2–1. We finish the season 14-8-1, and I am named All-American and Big East Rookie of the Year after setting a school record with fifteen goals and seven assists. But the bigger development for me comes when Glenn Crooks talks to Jerry Smith, the coach of Santa Clara, the reigning NCAA champion, and the newly installed coach of the U-21 national team.

"You need to take a good look at Carli Lloyd," Crooks tells Smith, underscoring how good a freshman year I'd had.

So Jerry Smith calls and invites me to camp. It is 2002 in Chula Vista, California, and it is terrifying. The team is loaded with big-name, big-time players such as Aly Wagner, Nandi Pryce, and Cat Whitehill, along with a goalkeeper from the Pacific Northwest named Hope Solo. It is the first time I meet Hope, and she is totally intimidating to me. She is strong and tough and has this air about her that she just might be in your face if you disagree with her about something or look at her the wrong way.

I do my best to only look at her the right way.

As scary as these players are to me, I caution myself to leave those feelings in the locker room. I know they won't do a thing for me on the pitch.

It works out.

"When players come into their first camp, there are certain things I am looking for — a mentality as much as anything," Smith says. "Everybody on a national team is a good athlete and most of them are skillful. What determines whether you are going to make it is the mental side, and that is what impressed me about Carli from day one.

"She played with a confidence that said, 'I have no fear. I don't have fear of success, and I don't have fear of failure. I can do whatever you want me to do. Now let's go.' After I watched Carli in her first full day, I said to myself, *Holy smokes, this kid just got here, and she isn't afraid of anything or anyone. She's taking people on. She's attacking the goal. She might just be the best player here."*

I have a bunch of things to work on, I know that. I am not the hardest-working player in the camp. I also have defensive deficiencies, mostly because all my coaches have just wanted me to sit in underneath the forwards, go on the attack, and let other players worry about it when the opponent has possession. But put the ball on my foot and point me toward the attacking third and watch me go. Jerry loves that defiance, and he tells the people at U.S. Soccer that I am somebody they need to invest in.

"Carli Lloyd isn't a finished product, but she's got stuff you can't teach," Jerry tells them. "This is a player we have to develop."

The mission of the U-21s is twofold. One is to work as a feeder for the full national team, and the other is to win the biggest international tournament of the year in that age group, the Nordic Cup, which is contested in northern Europe every summer. I make my first international trip for the United States, to Finland, in late July 2002, and though I don't get a ton of playing time, it is exhilarating to be part of a championship effort as we knock off Germany in the final. It is a significant step up the ladder for me, and when Jerry turns the U-21s over to Chris Petrucelli, then the women's coach at the University of Texas, I expect to climb a couple of more rungs.

Except that it doesn't happen that way. It's January 2003, and though I am coming off a second consecutive All-American year at Rutgers, I don't seem to be impressing my new coach when we have the first of our monthly camps in preparation for the Nordic Cup. He is on me constantly about my defense and isn't thrilled with my fitness level either.

I don't know what this guy's problem is, I think. *Every other coach I've ever had has appreciated what I can do, and this guy only talks about what I can't do.*

We move into March and then April, and I am not sure where I stand. The fearlessness that so impressed Jerry Smith has given way to doubts about where I fit in the scheme of the new regime. When we do drills, I know I am as good as or better than most everyone with my technical skill, and I can shoot from distance with anybody. I am scoring goals, but am I scoring any points with Chris Petrucelli?

At the close of the April camp, Chris is ready to name a roster of the players he is taking to Brazil for a pre–Nordic Cup tournament. He schedules meetings with every player. When it's my turn, we sit down in the lobby of the hotel where we are staying. It is handsomely appointed in spotless earth tones. People are milling about, doing what people do in lobbies, checking in, checking out. I am oblivious to all of it. My entire focus is on my coach and the report card he is about to issue. I believe in my heart that I should go to Brazil, but I don't know what to expect.

I brace myself for Chris Petrucelli's words. He starts to talk.

"You've done okay in our camps, Carli, but the truth is that you are not performing to the level of a national team player," Chris Petrucelli says. "It's not a lack of talent; you have plenty of talent. It comes down to a lack of effort — to your tendency to take time off during the flow of play, to not doing the work we need you to do defensively.

"In my role as the U-21 coach, they want me to develop the players we have to the point where I can say, 'I recommend this player for the national team.' And the simple fact is that you have not put yourself in a position where I can say that."

Chris Petrucelli finishes by telling me that I will not be making the trip to Brazil, or to the Nordic Cup.

He stands up, as if to signal the meeting is complete. I stand up too. I remember nothing else. I am in a daze. It is by far the most stinging evaluation I have ever received in my soccer career. Somehow I manage to avoid breaking down in front of him — I am not sure how — and slowly walk away. I honestly don't recall uttering an insincere "thank you," or wishing him a great day, or saying anything at all. I am so numb from this face slap that I can't even think.

I get back to my room and call my parents. They can barely hear me between the sobs.

"Chris Petrucelli just cut me from the U-21s. He says I'm not a national team player," I tell them.

My parents do their best to comfort me, they really do, but I can't take in any of it.

"I don't know if I want to keep doing this national team thing," I tell them. "It's not going anywhere. The players here are so good. The coach just finished telling me I'm not at that level. Maybe it's time to come home and just play out my final year at Rutgers and be done with it."

I fly home to New Jersey. I am sure I will never wear a USA jersey again.

Chris Petrucelli's rebuke is still singed into my psyche days before the U-21 team is about to leave for Denmark and the 2003 Nordic Cup. It feels really crappy to think about how I went to Finland with Jerry Smith's team a year ago and now here I am lying in my bedroom in Delran a year later, looking at my Ronaldinho poster and wondering how things got so fouled up. I haven't been with the U-21s for a couple of months. I have no idea what my soccer future is. I am at a crossroads, a midfielder in a muddle, and the more I think about it, the more I am convinced that it is time to give up the chase. As I told my parents, I will play my senior year at Rutgers, get a degree, and try to find a job. I mean, what's the point of putting in all the work on the field when clearly U.S. Soccer doesn't think I'm good enough?

If I can't stick with the U-21 team, how am I ever going to make the full national team? This is my belief, and don't try to talk me out of it. You've got no shot.

As I try to sort it all out, I find out that the U-21s are looking for a friendly game before they leave and have made arrangements to play a top Jersey club team that I sometimes play for. I am going to get to play against the coach who just told me I wasn't national team material.

Do payback opportunities get any better?

I figure I am on my way out of the U.S. Soccer orbit, but I don't mind leaving behind a few reminders of what might've been.

I don't have anything personal against Chris Petrucelli, not at all. I just want to show him that there's more to my game than he thinks. I don't work hard? I can't defend? I'm not national team–worthy?

I am all over the place in the friendly against my former team. I win fifty-fifty balls. I tackle hard. I go on the attack and generate threats. I don't remember the score, but I do remember that I bring it the whole game.

"Carli was a different player. Her overall commitment to playing the game was way different that night," Chris says.

The next day I get a call from the man who ripped my heart out, Chris Petrucelli. Kelly Wilson, an All-American forward for the University of Texas who had already played, and scored, for the full U.S. Women's National Team, suffered an injury in the friendly and won't be able to compete in the Nordic Cup.

"We need another player. Would you like to take the spot?" Chris asks.

"Yes, thank you," I say. "When do we leave?"

In the opening game, against host Denmark in the medieval city of Randers, Chris calls for me in the eightieth minute with the game still scoreless. We have been dominating, but the Danish goalie, Heidi Johansen, keeps coming up with huge saves. She is the keeper on the full Danish national team, and it isn't hard to see why. We finish the game with twenty-five shots, Denmark with three. The trouble is, we are not finishing them. The scoreboard says the game is tied, and that is all that matters.

"If you get a chance, go ahead and knock one," Chris says.

Almost instantly I get a chance, carving out enough space to drive a shot from the top of the box. Johansen knocks it down, and my teammate Lindsay Tarpley, the North Carolina star and national College Player of the Year, pounces on the rebound but knocks it just wide.

We keep pushing the attack. Seven minutes later, I beat a Danish defender and pound another shot, this time from twenty-five yards out. Johansen tracks it well, but the ball has too much pace to catch, so she deflects it away. Tarpley, again, is on the doorstep, picks up the rebound, and buries it. In just seven minutes, I have contributed two big scoring chances, the second of them an assist on the game-winner. It is something to build on, I hope.

We go on to beat Iceland, tie Norway, and come from behind on two goals by Joanna Lohman, our captain, to beat Sweden for our sixth Nordic Cup title in seven years. I am thrilled to be on the winning side, but frustrated that I play a total of only sixty-five minutes in the tournament. Being a late injury replacement, I realistically could not have expected more, but I head home full of more doubts than ever about where this is going. I am twenty-one years old. I am no better than a fringe member of the U-21 team, even though I've just been part of another Nordic Cup championship.

That is the truth. Why pretend otherwise?

I spend the rest of the summer training with the Philadelphia Charge of the Women's United Soccer Association (WUSA), thinking that this could be an option after I graduate.

I love to play soccer, and if the U.S. national team doesn't want me, maybe I will just play pro soccer, I think.

Then, in September, the entire league folds.

It feels as if doors are closing all over the place, and then things get even worse. Brian and I are out one night when he tells me, "I think we should stop seeing each other for a while."

My insides instantly go cold and numb. I briefly consider the idea that he might be kidding, but then I look into his eyes and realize quickly that he is not kidding at all.

Shocked? I am beyond shocked.

"Why do you say that?" I say.

"I don't know. I just think we need some space. You have a lot going on, and so do I. Things haven't been the same lately. It's just a gut feeling I have."

Brian and I had a breakup a few years before, just as I was starting at Rutgers. I was starting to travel a lot, and when summer came around he wanted to be with his friends, but somehow I never doubted we'd wind up back together. This time catches me much more off guard. Brian has just suffered the loss of a close friend, and that weighs heavily on him. I want to be there for him and support him, but I am devastated and mad, and not taking this news very well.

"Well, okay, if that's what you want, fine," I tell him.

I try to be brave, but I want no part of a separation, or space. This is the man I want to be with. I have no choice but to go along and trust that things are going to work out.

Brian and I stay in touch periodically, and I have a good year for Rutgers. We make it back into the NCAA tournament, drawing Maryland in the first round. I score on a one-timer in the first half, before the game ends in a 1–1 tie and we wind up winning on PKs. Next up is Penn State, ranked number six in the country, a team anchored by Joanna Lohman, my Nordic Cup teammate turned NCAA opponent. Joanna is such a good player, and a ferocious worker. She just goes and goes, and her level of play is as consistent as a metronome. I really admire that about her. You always know what you are going to get. Joanna scores early, and Penn State goes up two goals in the first six minutes. I blast a ball into the upper corner in the fourteenth minute, but we never can quite catch up, and then Joanna scores again in the eighty-fifth minute to make it 3–1. Our tournament, and season, are over, and my soccer soul-searching commences anew.

Three years into my Rutgers career, I've scored and assisted on lots of goals, won a bunch of honors, and helped turn us into a winning program. I am often mentioned in conversations about the top collegiate players in the country, and yet I still feel strangely unfulfilled.

I still feel like I'm an underachiever.

People have been telling me for years that I am going to wear a USA jersey someday, so how come I am going backwards? Were they just saying that to be nice?

Are Chris Petrucelli's words ("not performing to the level of a national team player") going to be my soccer epitaph?

Not long after my college season ends, I get a call from my father. He has just had an impromptu meeting with James Galanis of Universal Soccer Academy in the parking lot off of Ark Road in Lumberton. It was raining hard. James was packing soccer gear into his car, eager to get dry and get home. My father approached him and asked if he had a minute.

"I don't know if you remember, but you saw my daughter, Carli Lloyd, a couple of years ago when you were training one of her Medford Strikers teammates," my father said. "She's been on the U-21 national team and is looking to get back into the national program. Would you be willing to meet with her and, if you think it's a good fit, train her?"

James thought for a moment.

"I remember your daughter," he told my father. "If she is interested, tell her to give me a call."

"Thank you," my father said. "I will do that. I am sure she will be reaching out to you soon."

My father calls to share the news. I hear the excitement in his voice. He is convinced James Galanis is a trainer who can make a difference for me.

"He's an excellent trainer. I think you should at least talk to him and see what your take is," my father says. "It can't hurt, can it?"

"I'll think about it," I tell my father.

And I do think about it. Very slowly. A week passes. Another week passes. Thanksgiving comes and goes. I am still thinking. I'm not quite sure what my resistance is, but I am a little skeptical and a lot guarded. What are the chances that this guy is going to tell me something I haven't heard a hundred times before?

Why should I take the time to meet with a trainer who, however much he might know, is not working anywhere near the national team level? My honest feeling is that nothing is going to help at this point.

Finally, in early December, I call this James Galanis. He has such a thick Australian accent that I can barely understand him. I am standing up and pacing around my bedroom with the door closed, anxious to get the call over with. He asks me a few questions about my college season and my history with the U-21s. We set up a time to meet when I am home for winter break. Brian and I are back together again, and I am really excited to see him, and not so excited to see James. Brian and I plan a weekend trip to upstate New York to go skiing, but first I am scheduled to meet James, on a Thursday night on Ark Road. It's after eight o'clock when I pull into the lot in my little black Saturn. The temporary light stanchions cast a faint glow on the frozen field. James has set up rows of sticks and cones. This is his first up-close look at me in several years, maybe more.

"What do you say we start with some skill work and see where we are?" James says.

"Sure," I reply.

For the next hour, I audition for James Galanis. I juggle. I dribble in and out of the poles. I demonstrate my first touch, passing, volleying, my technique on the ball with every part of both feet. In between drills, James asks questions.

He asks more questions than any trainer I've ever worked with.

"Why do you think you were cut from the U-21s?"

"I don't know. I don't think I was the coach's type of player," I say. "He didn't seem to like me."

"What sort of teammate are you? Do you connect with people and support others?" he asks.

"That wasn't easy on this team. The team was full of cliques. It was hard to get any chemistry going. I don't think I really had a chance to show them the type of player I am."

"Do you like to go on the attack? What are your strengths?" James asks.

"I do like to attack and to take people on and send through balls, and I have a strong shot."

"Do you get back on defense at all?"

"No, I don't do that much. I just sit behind the strikers."

"Why?"

"That's what I'm best at. That's what my coaches want me to do," I say.

Almost every answer I give James is full of excuses, or buck-passing. The amount of ownership I take is negligible.

The session lasts for an hour. I am gassed about twenty minutes into it. I don't mind all the questions because they give me time to rest. When we're done, James says he wants to meet again on Saturday to do a fitness evaluation.

"This wasn't fitness, what we did tonight?" I ask.

"No, this was just an evaluation of your skill," he says.

I don't say anything. But all I can think about is what a mess I will be at the end of a fitness evaluation if I feel this way after I work only on skills. Still, there is something I like straightaway about James. He is very clear and direct. I like the questions he asks and the way he asks them. I like that he doesn't baby me. He hasn't talked about setting any standards or goals yet, but I can tell his are very high.

I report to our designated meeting place, on the track at Lenape High School in Medford, New Jersey, on Saturday afternoon. James says he wants me to do the Cooper Fitness Test, running at a steady pace for as far as I can go over twelve minutes.

"Without stopping?" I ask.

"Yes, without stopping," he says.

After a brief warm-up, I am ready, and off I go around the track, one lap and another and another. I want to stop, but I don't. I think I might throw up at one point but don't do that either. I finally finish up. Eight laps — two miles — is considered excellent. I don't even get to five — a mile and a quarter. All-American midfielder? Ha. My Cooper test is more worthy of a chain-smoker.

I look over at James, and he is not saying anything or betraying any emotion. His silence is making me nervous.

Next I have to do interval work, running 400 meters, then 200 meters and 100 meters. I go hard and do my best, but honestly, it's not very good and I know it. During the rest intervals, James asks more questions.

What's up with all these questions? I think.

When all the track work is done, I knock out as many sit-ups and push-ups as possible in two minutes, and then James asks me to sit down on the red bleachers. It's just the two of us at an otherwise deserted track. I feel as if I'm about to have the biggest exam of my life and hope I don't screw it up.

"So tell me, what do you want to do with your soccer career?" he says.

"I want to play for the U.S. Women's National Team," I say.

James is quiet for a few moments. The quiet stokes more anxiety. Part of me wonders if he is going to laugh, or at least tell me that I am in fantasyland.

Finally, James speaks.

"Okay, this is the story as I see it," he says. "Can you do it — make the U.S. Women's National Team? Yes, you can do it.

"Is it going to take a lot of work? It is going to take a whole lot of work. A whole lot. But if you put in that work, then I don't see any reason why you can't go as far as you want to go."

I take in his words and look up and down the red grandstand and then at this young Aussie guy a few feet away, with long dark hair and the thick-legged, athletic physique of a soccer player. I know very little about him, truthfully, but as I sit and listen to him I have an almost complete trust in what he is saying. I'm not sure I can even tell you why. He seems smart and very knowledgeable about the game, but more than that, he seems real. Usually it takes some time before I am ready to let my guard down around people I don't know well, but with James it happens almost instantly. I am encouraged for the first time in a long while. I want to hear more, and James obliges, providing the most detailed evaluation of me as a player that I've ever gotten.

It begins with him telling me about the Five Pillars, which he sees as the essential components of any world-class player.

"The Five Pillars are technical skill, tactical awareness, physical power, mental toughness, and character," James says. "To be an elite player you need to have them all. From what I see after this evaluation, you are strong in the first two. You are good on the ball and have skills that are very advanced. That's vitally important, because not many players have that. You also show a keen tactical awareness, and that's important as well.

"But the other three? Those are areas where you are sorely lacking.

You are not fit, and that's going to be a big challenge, because fitness does not come naturally to you. Mentally, you are weak. You don't push yourself hard and you are lazy, and you aren't the sort of player who is going to thrive under pressure. And your character? That is poor. You make excuses and find people to blame and don't want to look at your own role in things. You always have a reason why things are not working out, instead of focusing on what you can do to make them work out."

James Galanis has pretty much just shredded me, and somehow I am fine with it; I am not defensive at all, because I know he is 100 percent right. I don't argue or push back on anything he is saying. It is almost as if I've been waiting for someone like this my whole life.

He continues.

"If you keep working at 80 percent, you won't get anywhere," he says. "You need to stop with the excuses, and blaming this person, that person, and the man in the moon. You need to start treating every training session, every game, as if it were a World Cup final. You need to be the hardest-working person out there, every time, no exceptions. You can't just sit behind the strikers and feed them through balls and be a one-way player. You need to play box-to-box. You need to defend and do the dirty work. You complain about the coach not giving you enough time? You need to give the coach no choice but to give you time. That is what it will take, Carli.

"So here's the deal: soccer needs to be number one in your life. Not your boyfriend or your social life or anything else. Soccer. That's what it will take. If it's not number one, let's go home right now, because it won't work and we will be wasting our time. If I call you at 10:00 PM on a Saturday night and say, 'Meet me at the field in a half-hour,' I don't want to hear, 'Sorry, Coach, I am at a party.' You turn around to your friends and say, 'Sorry, everybody, but I have to go train.' You have to be ready and willing to train on Christmas and Easter and Thanksgiving, and all the other days that other people are resting. That's what kind of commitment it's going to take. If you are willing to make these sorts of sacrifices, I will be happy to work with you. I will do everything I can to help you reach your goals, because I know you have a lot of ability and I believe you have greatness in you. It is up to you. We have to build this foundation, day by day. We have to build on the strengths you have and get to work on the things you don't have. If you're ready, then let's get to work."

My head is spinning, but it's spinning in a good way.

"When do we start?" I ask James Galanis.

Climbing into my Saturn, I feel as though I've just gotten an IV infusion of hope. Everything is looking up suddenly. It's not just the prospect of working with James. It's being back with Brian too. We bumped into each other at a party and talked for a while. It was natural and easy, and soon we reconnected. Being with Brian is where I want to be, where I always want to be. I share with him the news about James and what a difference I think he can make.

"You only get one shot at this. I'm glad you are going for it," Brian says.

4

National Attention

I DON'T KNOW IT AT THE TIME, but James Galanis and I have much in common. As a player, he was a tough-tackling midfielder who could score from distance. He could slice balls deftly and pin balls near and far and change fields with a fifty-yard crossfield ping, just like me. And like me, he grew up in a working family that knew nothing about privilege or abundance.

James's parents come from a region in Greece called Symou, and neither of them had it easy. His father was the oldest of seven children, after his parents lost their firstborn child to illness. He dropped out of school in fifth grade to help his father — James's grandfather — with his work in a small general store on a mountaintop. James's mother dropped out a year earlier, in fourth grade, to work in the tobacco fields. With the economy in postwar Greece in a shambles, James's parents joined a massive wave of Greeks who emigrated to Australia to get a fresh start. His father was eighteen years old when he left his homeland, his mother sixteen. They lived only ten kilometers apart in Greece but never met until they both arrived in Melbourne. After falling in love and getting married, they raised a family in a little hardscrabble town called Preston.

James's father found work in a factory, dying fabrics. His mother worked as a seamstress and later started an office-cleaning business.

James was the middle of three children, and the language spoken at home was Greek. James still spoke no English by the time he got to be school age, which of course made for a miserable experience in an Anglo-dominant school. Other kids teased him. The teachers were frustrated with him because he couldn't understand English. James couldn't stand school and hated the way it made him feel. The only thing that saved him was soccer. James started playing at an early age at a park a short walk from his house, next to a public library. He picked it up quickly, and when he got a little older, his soccer skills made him popular both at school and in the neighborhood. Suddenly he wasn't the dumb Greek kid anymore; he was the kid you wanted to have on your soccer team.

James had two idols as a youngster. One was Diego Maradona, and the other was Bruce Lee. James was fascinated by the martial arts. When he discovered there was a top karate school, named Goju Ryu, right near his house, he would go there and sit on the steps outside and watch. One day when he was about eleven someone invited him in and introduced him to an instructor.

"If you like karate so much, why don't you just join the club?" the instructor asked.

"My parents can't afford it," James said.

"Mate, tell your parents if they pay $16 for a uniform, you can train for free," the instructor said.

James got his uniform, and from then on, if he wasn't on the soccer field, he was in karate class, working his way up through the ranks — white, yellow, green — until he finally made it to black belt. At age fifteen, his instructor entered him in a tournament. James had no idea what was at stake or who he would be competing against. He showed up and won his first fight, and then his second and his third, and wound up making it to the state championship.

James's karate training taught him about discipline, hard work, and the importance of technique — breaking skills down to specific components and then executing them flawlessly to get the desired result. It also taught him about the power of the mind, as he learned to meditate and visualize what he wanted to do in his bouts.

The rigors of his karate training did nothing but help James's soccer. He began playing with a local adult team at age fifteen, getting paid to play by a club called Clifton Hill. Over his parents' vehement objections, he dropped out of high school at sixteen to play soccer.

"My father didn't talk to me for two weeks, but I knew this is what I had to do," James says. "School didn't stimulate me. I had to get out of there."

James studied to be an electrician's apprentice, but mostly he played soccer, getting paid on a per-game basis and earning a reputation as one of the premier players in the area. During one off-season, in 1992, he decided to visit his parents' homeland and stayed on the island of Poros, where he met a group of other young people, including a college student from South Jersey named Colleen. She was on vacation from studying for her master's in business administration. Colleen and James were attracted to each other. Things proceeded slowly at first, but then James came to the States during the 1994 World Cup, and the romance took off. James spent the next few years splitting his time between Australia and South Jersey, heading to the States when his soccer season was over and staying for three months or so, then traveling the 10,000 miles back home for another season. All the crisscrossing of the world got old, and after James and Colleen got married, they decided to settle in South Jersey, where James started coaching and ultimately launched his own business, Universal Soccer Academy, in 2000.

I am not James's first soccer pupil, but I quickly become a regular. I start training with James almost immediately after the evaluation. When the subject of what the training would cost comes up, James is typically straight up. He never forgot what the karate instructor did for him, I guess. It is time to pay it forward.

"I am not going to charge you anything," James says. "I will spend as much time working with you as you want, because I believe in you. All I ask is that this be your number-one priority. As long as that is the case, I will be here whenever you need me, for as long as it takes."

Apart from being a great soccer trainer and a black belt, James

Galanis might be as good a long-range planner as I have ever seen. He doesn't tell me right away, but soon after we start working together he maps out a three-phase master plan for me. Phase 1 (2004–2008) is getting me well entrenched with the U-21s and into the mix with the full national team. Phase 2 (2008–2012) is continuing to improve my fitness and sharpen my overall game and solidify my standing on the U.S. Women's National Team starting eleven. Phase 3 (2012–2016) is to become a dominant player for the U.S. — and the best player in the world.

It is good he doesn't share this with me, because it might make my head explode. You don't start fixating on the finish line of a marathon when you're steps into the first mile.

Suddenly, the entire focus of my soccer life has shifted, and the biggest impact is on Brian. I am training with James four or five times a week, often two sessions of three hours apiece. Once I am back in school at Rutgers, I make the 100-mile round trip down to South Jersey more times than I can count. James says soccer has to come first, and he isn't kidding. If I am not actually working out with James, I am texting with him or talking to him about our workouts, or I am off doing fitness work. That typically happens at Laurel Acres Park, which has a stocked fishing lake, picnic grills, and five ball fields. I am not there to recreate. I am there to punish my body into shape. I do repeat sprints up the big hill that is Mount Laurel's top sledding location. I run the hill forwards, and backwards. And occasional suicides. It is a killer supplement to the distance running I do on the streets. James wants me to be able to run ninety minutes. That is what I am pushing for. I am going hard, all the time, and it's no different when I hop in on the training sessions James has with his Medford Strikers team, the Scream. James and I talk about the Five Pillars constantly. The pursuit of the Pillars rules my life. Brian takes the brunt of this — and his selflessness is staggering.

It's not easy when you have a boyfriend you love and you are spending most of your time away from him. Nor is it easy when you text and talk much more with your trainer than you do with him.

Brian is an athlete and a competitor and knows as much as anyone about the singular focus that is required. Not once does he give me a hard time when I go off to train or am away for a tournament, or when I tell him I can't go to a party or out on a date. One year his sister's wedding is right in the middle of a national team camp.

"I hate that I won't be there with you, but there's nothing I can do," I tell him.

"I know. I understand," Brian says.

I am away on his birthday, July 14, just about every year. When he graduates from golf school, the Golf Academy of America–Orlando, I miss that too. Lots of people would say they understand and then get resentful. Brian is as understanding as anyone I've ever known.

"I know this is your dream and whatever you have to do to make it happen, I'm fine with. I want you to be happy," he says. His devotion is so total that it might seem almost corny, or not of this world. Trust me, it is not corny, or fake. It is who Brian Hollins is.

It makes me love him that much more.

I am invited to Chris Petrucelli's U-21 camp in 2004, and right from the start I feel as though I am a different player. I am not a pretender anymore. I am not even just a contender. At each monthly camp we have, leading up to the Nordic Cup, I am emerging as a leader, even in the eyes of the coach who stomped on my dream about nine months earlier.

"It was as if Carli had become a different person," Chris Petrucelli says. "I didn't know her that well at that point. I don't know what she was doing a year before, but it was clear that soccer had become her ultimate focus. You saw it every day. It was like she became a pro. Lots of kids out there say, 'I want to be on the U.S. national team.' Then there are kids who say, 'I'm willing to do whatever it takes to be on the U.S. national team,' and that's where Carli was."

In late March we embark on a trip to China to play three games in the greater Shanghai area. It is the first of my many trips to China, and it is a body-clock shock, a culture shock, a diet shock. Honestly, if I had gone to Mars, I don't think it would be as much a jolt. I am so amped up I can't even sleep on the flight over, so I binge-watch movie after movie on my portable DVD player. I am seriously jet-lagged when we land in Shanghai, of course, and that only heightens the sensory bombardment. I'm a Jersey girl, so I am used to crowds, but I have never seen anything like this. The whole city seems to be in a near state of gridlock, and when it's not, cars will go anywhere and do anything. Tailgating is practically a sport. Pedestrians are treated as if they are a civic nuisance, of barely more concern than construction cones.

It is the grayest, grimiest place I've ever seen, the smog thick, the air smelly, with many people walking the streets in masks. Got to go to the bathroom? No worries. Most little kids I see wear these outfits where they can just undo the butt part of it, open a flap, and pee right there on the street. How convenient. Food is another adventure. I am finicky to begin with, and with offerings of dog meat and pigs' feet and other mystery items, I am completely grossed out. I eat mostly bread and grains and any fruit or vegetable I can find. Put it all together, I am not even close to being in my comfort zone, but thankfully the soccer part of the trip is much more agreeable.

I score a goal in a 4–0 victory over a top club team in the first game, and then we travel to the city of Jiangsu, not far from the Yangtze River, to play the Chinese women's national team. When we walk out, I am stunned by the sight before me. About 10,000 people are in the stands, nearly all of them wearing black or gray clothing. It is by far the biggest crowd I've ever played in front of. It makes me nervous. I keep looking up at all these people, a monochromatic sea of fans who are mostly quiet and polite, and I can't fathom that they are all there to see us play. The fans in Jiangsu do not get a whole lot to cheer about. I open the scoring in the eighteenth minute, and then feed our striker, Natasha Kai, who scores another goal two minutes later.

We win all three games and return home, and I'm happy with how things go and delighted not to look at a cut of meat and wonder if it's a dog. We continue with our monthly camps in preparation for the Nordic Cup in July. When I am not there, I am working faithfully with James, who more and more is drilling me on the psychological piece of this. It is so easy for me to lose faith and doubt myself and let little things distract me. Being aware of such tendencies is the first defense to reining them in. James helps me see that I don't have to listen to those self-critical and negative tapes that might be playing in my head. I have a choice. I don't have to go there. It's hard to break an ingrained habit, but being able to see it and step outside yourself and catch it is the way to start.

In one camp session, I struggle with my first touches and get stripped a few times. I don't have the right weight on several passes, resulting in giveaways. It doesn't take much to set my head spinning and get the doubts firing up. I am disgusted that I am not playing up to my level. James is working hard with me on not being overly self-critical and not listening to those voices when they show up. With his guidance, I constantly remind myself:

Just because you might have those thoughts doesn't mean you have to pay attention to them.

Just because you have them doesn't mean they are true.

"If you make a mistake, forget it and get on to the next play, the next touch or pass or tackle. Be the hardest-working player out there, always," James says.

In our April camp I get a chance to play with some national team players, and at the end of the month my phone rings. It is April Heinrichs, coach of the U.S. Women's National Team.

"The whole national team staff, along with Chris [Petrucelli] and his staff, have been very impressed with your ability and your potential to grow as a player at this level," April says. "We'd like to invite you to train with the full national team next month in Carson, California."

I am not expecting this. I am so thrilled I have a hard time finding the words, before stammering out a few.

"Thank you so much, Coach. It will be an honor to be there."

I have final exams coming up at Rutgers, but as much as I know it's important to get my degree, my entire focus is on Carson. When I walk out on the field for the first time, I know I will look around and see players such as Mia Hamm, Kristine Lilly, Briana Scurry, Julie Foudy, and Joy Fawcett. I know I will be as nervous as I've ever been in my life.

Calm down, Carli. They are soccer players, the same as you, I tell myself.

It doesn't work.

I mean, these are legends of the sport. I have their posters and autographs. I don't know what to call them or how to interact with them. Do I walk up to Mia Hamm and say, "It's an honor to be on the field with you"? Am I supposed to act as if I am a peer? I don't know. April Heinrichs is super-nice and welcoming. I hope as I prepare to take the field that the players are the same way.

Two of the first people I meet are Shannon MacMillan and Tiffeny Milbrett, two very gifted forwards. They could not be nicer.

"It's great to meet you and have you in camp," Shannon says. "I remember when I came into my first camp. It's not easy, but once you settle in and play your game, you will be fine."

Tiffeny is the same way. She greets me warmly. She feels genuine. "Let me know if you need anything," she says. I find out quickly that Shannon and Tiffeny are more the exception than the rule, because from the outset most everybody else is somewhere between aloof and downright chilly.

I am reserved to begin with, not someone inclined to be chatty in new situations, but the atmosphere makes me that much more of a loner. Almost nobody introduces herself. I'm not expecting a basket of fruit, but I barely even get acknowledged. I get the feeling that they would much prefer it if I were not there. Heather Mitts, a friend and longtime national team defender, tells me later she had the same experience when she first came on. So does Danielle Fotopoulos, a reserve on the 1999 World Cup championship team and another player in the 2004 camp who goes out of her way to make me feel a part of things.

"Don't take it personally, because it's not about you in the least," Danielle says, before sharing a story about her own early years, when she was sitting in the locker room, not far from a veteran team member who did her best to ignore Danielle. A few other newcomers came in, and the vet still wasn't talking. Then another longtime player showed up and the veteran suddenly turned into Ms. Sociable.

"Finally, somebody who I actually care about," the veteran player said.

When I hear this story, I make a promise to myself: If I ever make this team, I am not going to freeze out the young players this way. I am going to treat people with civility, the way they should be treated —even someone who plays my position.

It's not only the nice thing to do. It's the right thing to do.

It feels as if it's a girls' club, and no, new members are not exactly welcome. It's a strange dynamic when you get to the national team level, and it's probably this way in every sport. There are very few spots on the team, and the competition to get them is wicked. Anyone new who shows up is viewed, to some degree, as the enemy. That goes double if you prove yourself on the field and draw praise from coaches. I wish it were not that way. To me, it should all be a meritocracy, with everything coming down to what you do on the field. If you deserve a spot because of your play on the pitch, that should be the only criterion that matters. I am not naive; I know there's politics, that some people have private agendas, that coaches might be looking out for players they have a history with. I totally get that. I just think it's pretty small-minded to try to keep the club closed to newcomers, as if that could ever work.

April is extremely positive and encouraging to me, praising my technical skills and first touches, so no doubt that makes me even more of a persona non grata. I do my best to put it all out of my mind and play, but it isn't easy. The pace of play is so fast—faster than any field I've ever been on. All around me are world-class athletes who are on you in a second, primed to pounce on every loose touch. I feel as though I am barely able to keep up. One day we are playing 5 v. 5, and I am on Briana Scurry's team.

"You've got to do better than that," she snaps when somebody gets around me.

I get a glare and another dressing-down from Mia Hamm, who doesn't like the pace and location of a pass I make to her.

"C'mon! That's not a ball I can do anything with!" she says.

I know I'm on the field with the best players I've ever played with, and it's going to be an adjustment. Nerves aren't helping. I do my best to let the criticisms come and go.

Remember what James said, I tell myself. *Be the hardest-working player out there. Leave it all on the field. Every practice is a World Cup final.*

On a day when we're supposed to do fitness training — a series of punishing 800-meter runs — several team leaders get together and complain to April that it's too much strain on their bodies and the fitness work needs to be called off.

The players get their way. People have told me that the inmates run the asylum on the women's national team. Here is the first example of it I've encountered. It's hard for me to believe that the players have the ability to dictate to the coach, but apparently that's how things work.

I work hard and take chances, and I shoot from distance whenever I have an opening. Even when I am nervous and insecure, I always have confidence in my ball-striking. It is my calling card. Early in camp I rip a shot from thirty yards out that sails high but has a lot of pace on it.

"Wow," I hear a couple of the veterans say. April notices too.

"There were a lot of conversations among the staff about how well Carli strikes the ball," April says. "It was so technically perfect, with both feet, and that is so rare, even at this level. Her long-range passing was a real separator too. Lots of players can make the short-range pass, but Carli can hit it with precision fifty yards across the field.

"The more I watched her, the more I saw that the way she strikes the ball, dead center, makes it move in a way that is very difficult for a goalkeeper to handle. It reminded me of Michelle Akers. Here was a kid in her first national camp, and she struck the ball better than almost anyone who was already on the team. It was impossible not to see that."

I don't make the eighteen-player roster for the Athens Olympic Games later that summer, but I never really expected to. (April tells me much later that I was one of the final cuts and that if I'd been in camp a little longer I would've made it.) I shift my focus to another Nordic Cup for our U-21 team, this time in Iceland, where the water smells like sulfur and the scenery and hot springs are divine and it almost never gets dark, at least not in July. We cruise again, beating all four opponents by the same 3–0 score. I score from distance to finish off Germany and put us in the final, and then we crush Sweden for the championship.

The much bigger women's soccer tournament of the summer, though, takes place in Athens. The U.S. wins the gold medal on a diving header in overtime by Abby Wambach, a 2–1 victory over Brazil that is the final international game that Mia Hamm, Kristine Lilly, Julie Foudy, Brandi Chastain, and Joy Fawcett will ever play together. It's truly the end of an era, and twenty-four-year-old Abby is figured by many people to be the team's next breakout star, the player who will keep the U.S. on top.

I am six months into my work with James, and as much progress as I've made in that time, I am impatient that it hasn't happened faster. Twenty-year-old Lindsay Tarpley is a lethal hybrid forward/ midfielder, a rising star who scored the first goal in the final. Aly Wagner is twenty-two, but she's been a U.S. Soccer golden girl since she was a teenager; an attacking midfielder of the future with transcendent skills and vision, she's another 2004 Olympian.

Where does this leave me? Why does there have to be a talent clog in the exact position that I play?

In national team camp one day early, I am sitting alongside Danielle Fotopoulos in a van on our way to training.

"I've been working so hard for the last five or six months to get ready for this," I say. "I feel like I'm not even getting a look. Sometimes I don't feel like I'm getting anywhere."

Danielle looks at me like a kindly older sister.

"You have to try to be patient, Car," Danielle says. "Five or six months is just warming up. It is nothing in the big picture of things. This is hard, and you can't forget that. It doesn't happen all at once, and you can't expect it to and can't let yourself get frustrated by that.

"It just takes time. Even Mia Hamm was a backup for a number of years. You just have to make up your mind that you are going to outlast everybody else, and then you will be exactly where you want to be."

I think about Danielle's choice of words . . . *outlast everybody*.

I like the way they sound.

For me, soccer was love at first kick.

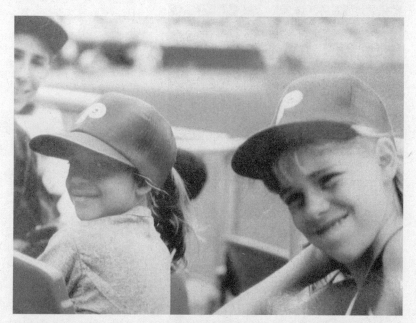

I've loved the Phillies since I was a little kid. That's me on the left, with my cousin Jaime Schoeffling Bula, at old Veterans Stadium.

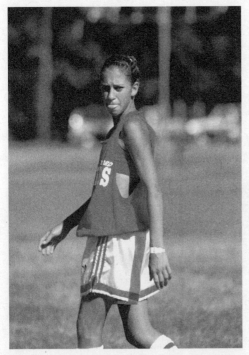

The Delran Dynamite helped get me on my way, thanks in large part to coach Karen Thornton and her assistant coach, Steve Lloyd, my dad.

Playing for the Medford Strikers was one of the best times in my soccer career.

Making the Olympic Development Program Region I team was a big deal for me as a thirteen-year-old kid. I'm the runt in the front row holding the plaque.

Family of five: the Lloyds of Delran. From left to right: my dad, my sister Ashley, my brother Stephen, me, and my mom.

The early years training with James Galanis. I call him the Wizard because there's nobody like him.

On the attack in my days with the Rutgers Scarlet Knights. (If you think I don't look as lean or fit as I am now, you are right.)

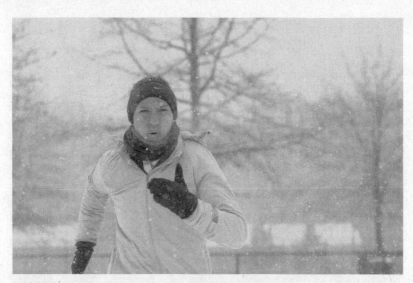

There's no such thing as a snow day when it comes to getting in my training.

My closest friends, Heather Mitts and Hope Solo, and I took a climb up the Great Wall of China before we got down to the business of soccer at the Beijing Games.

My longtime teammate and fellow midfielder Shannon Boxx and I are all smiles before a game at the 2010 Algarve Cup in Portugal.

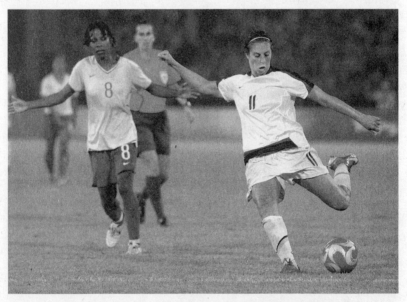

There's no sweeter feeling in soccer than scoring at a big moment. Here's the strike that beat Brazil in the 2008 Olympic gold medal game in Beijing. That's Formiga looking on.

Then-coach Pia Sundhage had open arms after I scored the game-winner against Brazil in Beijing.

My mom and dad (behind me at right) and most of our family gathered at the Philadelphia airport to celebrate after we won gold at the 2008 Olympics in Beijing.

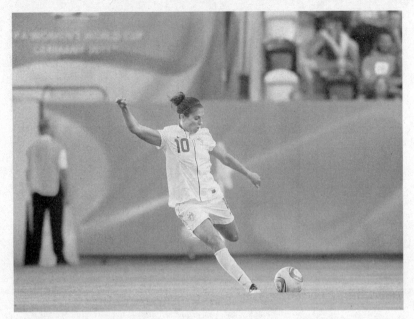

We gave it our all against Japan in the 2011 World Cup final in Germany, a heartbreaking loss in PKs.

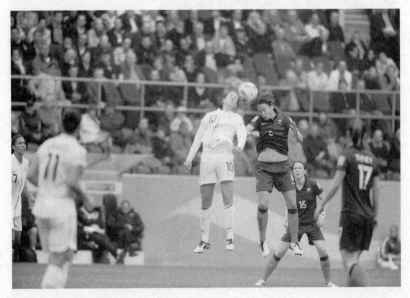

France, one of the best teams in the world, gave us a battle in the 2011 World Cup semifinals.

5

One Cap at a Time

IT'S AN IDYLLIC SUMMER SUNDAY in Portland, Oregon, six days before my twenty-third birthday, in one of the prettiest soccer settings in the United States. The date is July 10, 2005. The U.S. Women's National Team is about to take on the Ukraine at Merlo Field on the campus of the University of Portland. The day's dominant story line centers on Tiffeny Milbrett, a hometown girl who starred at Portland before going on to a superb career as a high-scoring forward for the national team. Tiffeny is one goal shy of 100 for her career, and what would be better than for her to reach the milestone here at home?

Everybody hopes Tiff gets it done and cooperates with the story line, though the truth is that I am preoccupied with my own milestone, albeit a much humbler one. Several days earlier, at the end of a training session in a national team camp I'd been invited to, Greg Ryan, April's assistant who had just replaced her as the national team coach a few months earlier, gathered everyone together.

"It's been a good camp. Thank you all for your hard work," he says. "Okay, this is the roster we're going to go with for the Ukraine match."

I feel as if I've had a good camp, but I've already learned that you can't take anything for granted when it comes to the national team, whether it's being invited to camp or making a roster cut. I've gotten really good news from coaches, such as when April invited me to my first full national team camp fourteen months earlier. I've also gotten really bad news, such as when Chris Petrucelli sent me home from the U-21s.

Greg starts to read the list. I am on the outskirts of a circle of players around him. I can barely stand the anticipation. Greg begins with the team captain — Kristine Lilly, of course.

He goes on, running through a familiar group of names, in alphabetical order: Fotopoulos ... Markgraf ... Milbrett ... O'Reilly ... Tarpley ... Wagner ... Welsh.

Somewhere in the middle he says:

"Lloyd."

Did I hear that right? Lloyd?

Did Greg Ryan just announce my name?

Yes, he did.

Truly, he did.

I look around the field, and it's almost as if a tidal wave of euphoria is going to sweep me away. How often in life do you think and dream about something for so long — in this case more than half my life — and then have it come true?

I am on the U.S. Women's National Team. I am not just in the camp, not just being checked out. I am on the roster.

I am in disbelief.

I can't wait to share the news with James. I can't wait to tell Brian and my parents.

The equipment manager comes over and tells me I need to pick out a uniform number. I am given the available options and decide on 22 because my cousin Jaime wore it. (I will change to 5 for my second game, and later switch to 11, before getting the number I wanted all along — 10.)

I don't wear Jaime's clothes anymore, but I still want to be like her.

The night before the game, I am a nervous wreck. I wonder if I am even going to be able to play. Will I trip on a bootlace running out for warm-ups? Will I be able to make a touch without knocking it halfway to Mount Hood? I call James for reassurance; I know he'll say the exact right thing because he always does. We've been working together eighteen months, and he knows my psyche better than I do.

"It's the same game and you are the same player," James says. "Think of all the training we've done to get to this point. I guarantee nobody on the team has put in greater effort or commitment to get to this position.

"Don't overthink it. Just go out and play. Let your training do the talking. If the coach calls for you, keep it simple in the beginning and take more and more risks as things go on. No matter what, be the hardest-working player on the field and walk off knowing that you emptied the tank."

Before we hang up, James has a few final words.

"Whether you play the full ninety or you don't play at all, I am proud of you — as a student and as a person. Remember, this is just the starting point. We are going to keep working, and you are going to get better and better and better."

James's words are a big comfort, but I still have a restless night of sleep and can't stop thinking about what it will be like to put my kit on and see the 22 jersey with the name LLOYD on top of it. My friends Nandi Pryce and Danielle Fotopoulos take turns trying to calm me down. In the pregame, I feel completely gassed just doing basic warm-up drills; my adrenaline is running on overdrive, burning through my energy supply.

I take a seat on the bench, and it doesn't take long to figure out this is not going to be a game full of drama. Early in the second half, we are already up 4–0 when Aly Wagner, our attacking midfielder, chips a perfect ball to Tiffany, who is making a run on the left side. Tiffany controls and sees that the Ukrainian keeper, Veronika Shulha, is well off her line; she pops a left-footed ball over Shulha's head into the unguarded net, an artful goal from an artful player. The crowd goes nuts, and Tiffany celebrates and cradles the ball that makes her only the sixth U.S. woman to reach the 100-goal mark. Just one year earlier, she had quit the team over philosophical differences with April. When Greg Ryan took over, he brought Tiffany back. It's an important reminder that every coach views the game differently and that different coaches have their own flavor preferences when it comes to players.

You can't control a coach's preferences, but what you can do, as James never tires of telling me, is make up your mind to outwork everybody.

A minute or two after Tiffeny scores her historic goal, Greg Ryan looks down the bench.

"Carli, start warming up," he says. I peel off my warm-ups and begin the soccer substitute ritual, stretching and twisting and running, back and forth over the same sliver of sideline. At the next stoppage of play, Greg tells me to go in for Aly. I am standing on the edge of the Merlo Field pitch, trying to breathe and remembering James's words.

Just go out and play. . . . Let your training do the talking. . . . Keep it simple.

Play finally stops. It is the sixty-fourth minute.

Aly comes off, and I give her a quick hug and run out into the midfield. Play resumes. I get involved quickly. I make a couple of tackles and connect on a few short passes. The nerves gradually recede. Soon I am not first-cap Carli anymore — I am just a soccer player. (A "cap" is an on-field appearance with the national team.) Minutes go by and I start taking more risks, making a backheel pass and taking on people. As time winds down I beat a defender and make a quick run up the middle and thread a ball to Heather O'Reilly, a fellow New Jerseyan and the youngest player on the team. Heather has already scored not more than a few minutes earlier, and it looks as if this might be another one, but her shot goes just wide.

The referee blows the whistle three times, signaling the end of the match, and as Tiffeny Milbrett gets ready to be honored and interviewed by the press, I grab a ball to commemorate the occasion. Everybody signs it. Somebody writes, "The first of many." I like the sound of that.

Even before my first cap, 2005 is shaping up as a game-changer of a year. A new coach takes over the U-21s, and I get an invite to training camp in preparation for another Nordic Cup. (The rules allow each team to bring in a couple of over-age players, and I am one of them.) The coach's name is Jill Ellis. She has a great reputation, having built UCLA into a national power that went to seven straight College Cups. Being on the West Coast, Jill doesn't see the top players in the East that much, so she consults with Julie Shackford, the Princeton coach and Jill's best friend, to get the rundown.

"Julie was always telling me about this player at Rutgers who would carve them up when Princeton played them," Jill says. "She said, 'She's a one-man wrecking crew. Her name is Carli Lloyd and she just takes us apart.' So that was the first time I heard Carli's name."

When Jill took over the U-21 team, she checked back with Julie and asked her if she should bring me into camp.

"Oh my gosh, yes. You definitely want to bring her in," Julie said.

Jill tells me later that she was intrigued by my technical proficiency and comfort on the ball, and by my ruggedness. She is the daughter of a renowned British soccer coach, John Ellis, who moved the family to Virginia when Jill was fifteen. Jill grew up playing and coaching in the Northeast — Region I of the Olympic Development Program.

"From the beginning I noticed that the kids from eastern New York and New Jersey, they just had this way about them," Jill says. "They had an aggressiveness, a confidence that bordered on arrogance, and I thought from the start that that was very apparent in Carli."

We steamroll through the Nordic Cup for a record seventh straight victory, beating Germany 3–1 in the third game to win our group and then blowing out Norway, 4–1, in the final. The German coach tells Jill that we are one of the best U-21 teams he has ever seen.

At seventeen years old, Lauren Cheney is a force up top and opens the scoring in the final, before I knock a ball to Heather O'Reilly, who freezes a defender with a stutter-step and drives a left-footer into the right side from twelve yards out to make it 2–0 early in the second half.

Cheney makes a nice cross to me about fifteen minutes later, and I knife through two defenders and toe-poke a shot into the corner for 3–0. I finish my best Nordic Cup with three goals and two assists in the four games, and not long after, I get my first payday as a soccer player — a $5,000 Athlete Support Grant from the U.S. Olympic Committee.

The money does not change my life. I do not immediately go out house- or car-shopping. Still, it's a huge deal to me, an affirmation that things are heading in a good direction and that I am actually finding my way into adulthood. I celebrate by buying a flat-screen TV for my room at home. I'm not home to watch it much, but it feels good to know I bought it with money I made from playing soccer. I am still a young woman in a big hurry, and I want this to happen now. It's almost a daily wrestling match to keep reminding myself of Danielle Fotopoulos's words of counsel at my first national team camp about how hard it is to break through, how you have to keep grinding it out — or, as James tells me over and over, how I have to keep emptying the tank every time I play.

It sounds as simple as tic-tac-toe, I know, but the whole process is fraught with so much anxiety at times that I need the constant reminders.

And nobody knows it better than James. Before every training camp or major competition, he writes me a long email, offering positive reinforcement and underscoring the same key themes. I read them over and over, hardwiring them into my brain. It's such a blessing to have a trainer who is so wise and giving, a trainer I can trust totally.

"All players at the national level have talent; it's the ones with character who end up making it," James writes before I head off to a camp in 2005. "Character that shows that you are willing to do whatever it takes to win. Character that shows that you will play as the coach asks and [you're] a player that gives the coach undivided attention when in the huddle and at team meetings. It is important that you show all these signs although they are not things you do with the ball.

"Make sure you show the coaches that you are there to be a winner and not another talent going to waste."

I get my second career cap in Charleston, South Carolina, where we play Mexico in a friendly in late October. I come on in the second half for Aly Wagner, and with a 3–0 lead already on the board (thanks to a goal by Kristine Lilly and two by Abby Wambach), I am ready to heed James's words and show character by doing whatever needs to be done to seal the victory. We have not allowed a goal for the entire year and don't want to mess this up in our final game of 2005, so we stay compact and fend off the Mexicans' attempts to get an attack going.

In the closing minutes, I am controlling the ball near the 18-yard line when I see Shannon MacMillan making a run on the right. I slip the ball through to her, and Shannon hits a hard shot that the Mexican keeper makes a kick-save on. About a minute later, it's my turn to fire, also from the right side of the penalty area. I hit a hard shot as I am knocked to the ground. The keeper blocks it, and I pop up and one-time the rebound, only to be stopped again.

The referee is about to blow his whistle to end it when I get the ball again, now about thirty yards out. I love to shoot from distance. It can't be anything but good for me to show Greg Ryan the kind of threat I can be in midfield. I take a full-throttle swing at the ball, coming through so hard that I completely lose my balance. The ball skies high enough that it could hit a seagull, and I go down. I land on my left wrist. I hear it crack. The whistle blows and the game is over, and I am off to see team doctors and get an X-ray. I don't need pictures to know what happened. My wrist is broken. The pain is throbbing. I am out for six weeks, and I am sick about it. The only good thing is that we have no more camps or games, so my bum wrist and I head farther south to spend time with Brian at golf school in Florida.

One doctor I visit thinks I should have surgery, but the U.S. Soccer medical staff is convinced that it will fully heal on its own and all I need to do is put a cast on it, which sounds good to me.

I want to get back training and playing as soon as I can because 2006 is going to be a big year. We begin with a January camp and a trip to China, the start of a process that will have a major impact on who Greg Ryan selects to play in the World Cup in 2007. I don't have a great read on what Greg thinks of me as a player. I do know that he has a defensive mentality and that I am going to have to prove to him that I am a full-service, two-way midfielder. The proving needs to start right away. I can't leave any doubt.

6

Coach's Crosshairs

I AM A WORRIER BY NATURE. I could've majored in over-thinking at Rutgers if it were an option. My default position is to re-play things as often as I dribble through little orange cones, which is often, and the matter that I am overanalyzing at the moment is this:

Why does Greg Ryan hate me?

Why is he always on my case, and why can't I ever seem to please him?

It's the beginning of 2006 and my wrist is healed, but my soccer self-esteem feels as if it's been flattened by an eighteen-wheeler. We have a camp in January, and I make the roster to travel to China for the Four Nations Cup, my first international trip with the full na-tional team. The good news ends there. I barely play at all, and when I do I feel as though Greg Ryan is all over my case, mostly about my defense.

That is his highest priority. He is a coach whose preferred style is lockdown defense on one end and bruising, direct offense on the other. I know how important it is to defend; I've known it ever since Chris Petrucelli cut me precisely because I wasn't up to his standards in that area. James has been pounding that into me from day one on Ark Road. Still, an attacking midfielder is supposed to attack, no? Shouldn't she be able to carve the defense up and spread the ball around the field and be a threat in the attacking third? Greg seems to be completely unimpressed with what I can offer when I am on the ball.

"You can't give her so much room."

"You can't stab in like that."

"You can't just play in one direction when you are in the midfield."

These are things I hear constantly from Greg Ryan, whose prototype of an ideal midfielder seems to be Shannon Boxx, who is very much a defensive-minded player. All I seem to hear is "Great job, Shannon," and, "Way to defend, Shannon," for weeks on end. The coach is right: Shannon is a defensive workhorse, and she is incredibly valuable because of that. I am not questioning that at all.

I *am* questioning where that leaves me with Greg Ryan, and so I commence with the overthinking, stressing over my lack of playing time and trying to figure out how I can change Greg's mind. I get back to the States, and James goes to work on me.

"Don't worry about what you can't control, mate," James says. "Just keep emptying the tank and getting better. Everything else will take care of itself."

So I get back into the office with James, but as I do I have some business stuff to sort out. I'm under contract with U.S. Soccer now and also have endorsement interest from Nike, Puma, and Adidas. The money is relatively modest, but symbolically it's another sign that I am no longer just a kid who loves the game; I am a professional soccer player. I know I need an agent to handle this for me, and it just so happens that Rich Fornaro, my mother's cousin, is an attorney. My mother works for Rich in his office in Hamilton, New Jersey. Rich is a sharp guy, a very likable guy. He has been handling some of the initial business offerings informally, but now it is time to firm things up. My parents have no doubt that Rich is the man for the job, and I'm good with it. "It's great that we can keep this in the family and have someone representing you who we can completely trust," my father tells me. Then he calls James.

"My wife and I have discussed it, and we've decided Rich has got to be the one to represent Carli," my father says. "He's a family guy, and my wife works for him, and it just makes sense all the way around."

James says, "That's fine with me, mate. As long as Carli is on board, we're good."

On a Saturday night in the spring, we all have dinner at Rich's house, a ceremonial closing of our working relationship.

After a little time passes, I am training with James, getting ready for the next camp, an important proving ground for me with World Cup qualifying beginning in the latter part of the year. I can't say I know exactly what the trigger is, but I've gradually begun to have some second thoughts about working with Rich. What if some problem or issue comes up? Could that jeopardize my mom's job? Wouldn't it be awkward for everybody? Couldn't it also wind up hurting me that he is not a sports agent and doesn't know the legal landscape in that area? I've had these endorsement opportunities for some time, and still no agreement has been reached.

I am also starting to question my parents' involvement — actually, overinvolvement. I'll always love them for all their sacrifices of time and money to help me, but now I am twenty-four years old, and more and more their input seems to put a strain on our relationship. When I come back from a camp, I am often grilled with questions. *How did you play? How was your body language? Did you connect with the other players?* These camps are exhausting and mentally grinding all by themselves. Having to give a full debriefing isn't something I have much patience for.

"I really don't want to talk about it," I say. "I just have to keep working hard."

This answer always sets my parents off.

The issue that my parents harp on above all others is making sure I play the political game, being nice and forging alliances with influential veteran players. I want to make the team because of my skills and not because of who I am friends with.

"I don't want to be a suck-up," I say.

"That's not what I'm suggesting. I just want you to be smart and give yourself your best chance to succeed," my father says.

I have never been somebody to go with the crowd. My parents appreciated that quality in high school when lots of other kids were partying and messing around with alcohol and drugs and I was getting sleep so I could be ready for my next training session. It's not about being antisocial or rude. It's about putting in the effort on the field and getting where I want to go. If that means missing out on parties or social events, hey, I'm going to do whatever it takes. My mother would caution me at times about being too much of a loner and not going out with my teammates.

"Mom, going out partying is not what's going to get me on the national team. Staying back and resting and being ready to kick ass the next day and showing the coach I'm emptying the tank — that's what is going to get me on the national team."

Briana Scurry, the great goalkeeper who helped the U.S. capture the 1999 World Cup, is my roommate on one of our road trips. I ask her if she talks to her family about her soccer career, and if they are involved at all in the business side of it.

"I never talk to them about any of it," she says. "I love my family, but they don't understand. I never want to mix family and business."

Bri has been around a lot longer than I have. Her point makes complete sense to me. I call James.

"I've been thinking it over, and I am not sure I want to go with Rich after all," I tell him. "I'm just not comfortable with it." I share about my conversation with Bri. I bring up my concern about what could happen to my mother's job if things don't go well. Most of all, I think it's important to have someone who has experience in the soccer world and knows the fine points of endorsement deals.

Nothing against Rich, but this is not his area of expertise. James knows Rich well and likes him as much as I do. He has coached Rich's son for years. James agrees that my points are valid.

"What are you going to do?" James asks.

"I'm going to tell Rich that I've been reconsidering things and I think I am going to explore other options," I tell him.

I reach out to Rich and explain my thinking. I tell him that I feel badly about changing my mind, but my gut tells me this is the right decision.

Rich is totally classy about it.

"I understand completely," Rich says. "You have to go with what makes the most sense and makes you most comfortable."

I am hugely relieved, but my parents are incensed. It's the first, completely independent decision I've made in my life and my parents think I've blown it big-time.

"I just don't want you to lose your job in case something breaks down," I try to explain to my mother. "At the end of the day I just think it's risky to mix family and business. I am just not comfortable with the entire thing."

Nothing I am saying is registering. None of us are very good at handling anger and other strong emotions. Like a lot of families, we wind up getting our backs up and our egos involved, and then listening stops and accusations start flying like shrapnel. I am as guilty as anybody.

I collect some stuff and storm out of the house and go to stay at Brian's. There's no way I want to sleep under this roof with all this hostility swirling around.

The situation isn't good, and James is concerned that if things fester, it will not only be terrible for the family but could also mess up my head and affect my performance. James has always had a very good relationship with my parents, dating to the rainy night three years earlier when my father approached him in the parking lot about working with me. For years, my father has praised James effusively and told me how fortunate we are to have a trainer of his caliber. That he has never charged us a nickel makes us that much more fortunate. James thinks it's important for me to sit down with my parents and try to explain things again and see if we can smooth over some of the anger and hurt.

"That's fine, but I'd like you to be there, because I don't think I'll be able to get my points across if you are not," I say.

James agrees, and we arrange for the four of us to get together for dinner at a place called Prospectors, a Western-themed steakhouse and dance hall on Ark Road, just down the road from James's training fields. Prospectors has photos of cowboys on the walls and a lineup of saddles along a saloon wall, and you almost expect Wyatt Earp to come barging through the door. It is a Monday night, at six thirty. The place is empty, but we get an out-of-the-way table anyway, just to ensure our privacy. I am trying to be positive, but the truth is I am dreading this because of how hard my mother came at me in our first conversation.

My parents and James are sitting at the table when I arrive. James says, "I don't enjoy being in the middle of a family issue, but Carli invited me and I want you to know I'm just here to help. I know you guys are upset about what's happened with Rich."

My father says to me, "I think what you did to Rich is wrong, but honestly that's not what we really care about. Our biggest concern is the way you disrespect your mother and me. It's almost like you're not the same daughter we raised and supported all these years." He gives a quick rundown of the times I've mouthed off, not answered calls or emails, kept them at a distance. I try to offer my side of things. My father keeps going, talking right over me.

My frustration is building by the second. Suddenly, I snap. I push back my chair and stand up.

"I came here to try to work things out, not to find out how terrible a person I am," I say. Then I storm out. It's not the most mature move of my life, but what can I tell you?

I told you I don't always do well with anger.

In the time it takes to click your spurs, a family fire has turned into a full-blown conflagration, my parents laying into me, me ripping right back. In that moment, I just feel hopeless, as if I'll never be heard or have my feelings respected. I feel bulldozed. I am so sad that it has come to this. I call Brian, and he comes and picks me up.

The fight in the corner of Prospectors stays with me a long time. We've had our spats before, sure, but this is a deeper cut. It's far beyond feeling rejected or misunderstood. I stick to my plan to look elsewhere for representation. I hire the services of John Johnson of Cozen O'Connor. It turns out to be one of the best moves I've ever made.

. . .

The next big tournament is the Algarve Cup in March in Portugal, and in the second of the four games Greg Ryan gives me my first start in a 5–0 rout of Denmark. I help set up one of Heather O'Reilly's two goals and feel pretty good about my performance. Greg is still on me a lot about my defense, but every day I show up and work, and I believe I am gradually winning him over. I start again in the final against Germany and bang a shot off the left post from distance in the first half. The game remains scoreless and goes to PKs, the Germans finally prevailing, 4–3. It stinks to lose, but it's impossible not to see that I am making progress. I just started two of four games — including the final — of one the most important competitions of the year.

A couple of days later, an email arrives from Greg. He is not an easy coach to read. His emotions and his assessments are about as stable as a weather vane in a windstorm. One day he might heap high praise on you. The next day he might act as if you're lucky you haven't been sent home already. I don't know Greg Ryan very well at this point; maybe this is a motivational technique, to keep his players uncomfortable. After Algarve, I am apparently on his good side.

"You had a fantastic tournament," Greg writes. "You should gain a lot of confidence from your performance in Portugal. Do not be satisfied as your potential is way ahead of you. Keep learning every time you step into a training session or a game. You have a great future with this team if you keep giving everything in you."

Greg's email is the most affirming assessment I've ever gotten from him. If only things were as positive at home. On the surface, my parents and I are getting along a little better, and I guess that is encouraging, but the deep, underlying divide remains. My parents are angry and resentful that I am closing them out of my soccer career, and I am angry and resentful that they refuse to let me take full ownership of my soccer career. I understand that our whole family life revolved around my travels and tournaments for years, and that my brother and sister got short shrift as a result.

It doesn't mean that my parents have lifetime rights to tell me what to do.

I keep trying to make this point, and it never seems to get through. This is my journey. If I fall, I have to be the one to pick myself up. If I'm not getting the playing time I want or not impressing the coach, it's up to me to figure out why. Having something go wrong doesn't mean it's time for a family discussion; it means I have to get better, make better decisions, and get back to the place that will take me where I want to go — back on the training field with James. If Greg is all over the place in his opinion of me as a player, I just have to work harder and eliminate any doubts he might have.

The problem with my parents is compounded by my father's frequent critiques of my game. My dad was my first coach, the coach who launched me on my way. Of course he wants me to do well, but sometimes it is too much for me to take in.

A week after my twenty-fourth birthday, we play a friendly against Ireland in San Diego. I fly my parents out and put them up in a hotel so they can watch the game. Shannon Boxx, a stalwart holding mid, is out with an injury, and Kristine Lilly is out too, so I know I am going to have to shoulder much more of the defensive responsibilities.

We come out flying, peppering the Irish goal with shots. In the twentieth minute, I slip a pass down the left wing to Christie Welsh, who crosses to a charging Heather O'Reilly, who knocks it in. Defender Cat Whitehill pounds in a rebound and we're up 2–0 at the half, on our way to a 5–0 victory.

I meet my parents briefly after the game.

"You didn't look like yourself," my father says. "You've gone away from the creative, attacking game you've always played."

"Dad, I'm playing the way the coach wants me to play. He wants me to be a ball-winner and be as active on defense as I am on offense," I say.

Neither of us is happy. The standoff continues.

I want to believe that I will resolve things with my parents eventually, but right now my focus is on firming up my spot on the roster and getting ready for World Cup qualifying. I have solid games starting in late-summer victories over China and Mexico and then earn my fifteenth cap in a friendly at the Home Depot Center in Carson, California, against Chinese Taipei. The game is October 1, 2006, almost a year to the day since the start of the World Cup in China, and it is not what you'd call a stiff challenge. We get off twenty-three shots, to none for Chinese Taipei. Abby Wambach records her fifth hat trick and adds three assists. In the seventy-sixth minute, with the score 7–0, Abby gets a ball with her back to the goal, about thirty yards out, and one-times the ball out to the right, where I am making a run. It is a perfect pass. I run onto it in full stride, fire, and slot it into the lower far corner. I make a little half-hop in delight — anything more would've been tacky given the score — and my teammates rush up to congratulate me.

It is my first goal for the U.S. Women's National Team, the biggest moment I've had since I made my debut in Portland fifteen months earlier. Not unlike that first cap, it is surreal to be in my boots, running back upfield, trying to get my head around the fact that I've just scored a goal for the United States of America.

Three minutes later, Megan Rapinoe, a rising, twenty-one-year-old star who is still a senior in college, follows with the first goal of her career (and adds number two a few minutes after that). It is our eighth straight victory after the PK loss to Germany in the Algarve Cup final, improving our 2006 record to 13-1-1. Everything would be looking great except that we head off to South Korea for three games and I am back in Greg Ryan's doghouse. We play Denmark in the first game, and the coaches tell me right before the game is starting that they want me to man-mark a Danish player. Almost from the first whistle to the last, Greg is yelling at me.

"You're giving her too much space, Carli."

"Tighten up on her."

"Carli, we need you to defend."

At halftime, Greg reams me out some more, and then says, "I'm going to give you another chance to go out there and get it right."

I work hard and think I mark the Danish woman pretty effectively, but Greg definitely does not agree. The game ends in a 1-1 draw, and we look awful. I don't play in the next game against Australia, and then we have a midfielders' meeting and Greg lets me have it one more time.

"Your defense is really hurting us. You are making us vulnerable over and over again, and it's got to stop," he says.

I don't mind being criticized and will listen to anything that I think will help make me a better player, but I honestly feel Greg is way off on this. I probably should keep my mouth shut.

But I don't.

"I think my defending is getting better. I don't think defending is our problem."

Greg glares at me, his face reddening. Now he is screaming at me.

"Your defending is horrible! You don't know what you are talking about! We looked like crap against Denmark, and if you don't see that you are clueless."

I am as angry as he is now. The meeting breaks up, and he tells me to hang around. It's just the two of us.

"Don't you ever question me like that again in front of other players," he says. "You have no right to do that. You make me look bad, and you make yourself look like a bad teammate, someone who thinks she is bigger than the team. You better knock it off or you are going to have a very short career with the national team."

I almost start crying on the spot but hold it together until I get back to my room, where I completely lose it and start bawling my head off. Even more than Greg's harsh words, what upsets me is that I have no idea where I stand with him. He changes moods and evaluations the way most people change socks.

I believe — I know — I am a better defensive player, a harder-working player, than I was back in the spring when he wrote me that glowing email. Am I really that much worse now? Am I going backwards, or is he trying to motivate me? I was totally, utterly wrong to mouth off — that only made things worse. I let my frustration get the better of me.

I have to do better.

• • •

I am back in the starting lineup for the last two games of the South Korea trip, and we win them both, against the Netherlands and Canada. Though I can never be sure, Greg isn't on me as much. We head back to the States and our home base, the Home Depot Center, for the biggest tournament I've played to date in my short time with the national team — the CONCACAF Gold Cup, which serves as the World Cup qualifier.

Our opener is against Mexico in late November, and I go the full ninety minutes in a 2–0 victory. Overall it is one of my best efforts yet. I defend well, tackle hard, and spray balls all over the park, one-touch passes here and through balls there. I ping balls across field and put pressure on the Mexican defense. Best of all, the victory assures us of a spot in the World Cup the following year in China. We finish the job by defeating Canada in overtime, 2–1, and it's a little extra sweet because James comes out to watch in person. It is great to have him there and meet everybody.

When James congratulates Greg on the Gold Cup victory, Greg has a moment with him.

"Please make sure Carli gets some time off and rests up. Next year is going to be a long grind," Greg says.

The team takes a holiday break, and I head back to South Jersey. I don't tell Greg, and I'm sure James doesn't either, but there's no way I'm backing off. A couple of days to recharge is all I need, and then James and I head for the Blue Barn, our winter training location in Marlton, New Jersey, a tin-sided place that sits off Tuckerton Road and looks as if it could double as an airplane hangar. I keep going back to the truth I learned when I started working with James: I am not naturally fit, so I need to do more physical training than just about anybody. I need to keep adding cords of muscles, build endurance, and sharpen and tighten all my ball skills.

Rest?

I don't think so.

7

World of Trouble

I HAVE TWO NEW BEST FRIENDS as 2007 begins. One is my roommate for yet another trip to China, Marci Miller. Seven years older than me, Marci is the big sister I never had, a person I immediately trust and connect with. Both of us are homebodies who don't care about going out and partying and hanging out until all hours. It's shocking to me, honestly, but there are lots of players who party hard. Marci and I have our own little film club; we stay back in the room, watch movies, and encourage each other constantly, even though we are both center midfielders and theoretically competing for playing time. I make fun of her when she goes out and buys a pair of Skechers. She makes fun of me for my tough, Jersey-girl game face.

Marci grew up in a blue-collar suburb of Chicago, so I guess it's no surprise that she is the ultimate blue-collar player. Her game is built on grit and ball-winning and sacrificing everything for the team. She is close to thirty years old when she debuts for the national team, making her one of the oldest rookies ever. As good a player as she is, Marci was never hailed as the future of the team. She has none of the entitlement or attitude that often accompanies the players who are touted that way. When we are not watching movies, we are tuning in episodes of *90210* and *Lost* and laughing a lot. Marci does her work and tries to find the best in everybody.

What is not to love about that?

Being with Marci is like being back with the Medford Strikers girls. She always has my back, the same way the Strikers did. Now that I've had a few years with the national team, I am witnessing a much different team dynamic, and often a much less pleasant one. I see people who seem to be threatened by me and aren't eager to see me do well because I might take their spot. I see a culture of wariness instead of warmth. Early in my time with the team, I make a run in the attacking third and am wide open and do not get the ball. I don't think anything of it, until it happens a second time, and then a third.

Finally, it dawns on me that I'm not getting the ball because this teammate does not want me to have it, never mind that I might do something good with it. No, the pass instead goes another way, from one friend to another. The realization is stunning to me, and sad.

Do players on the U.S. Women's National Team really make decisions on who they pass to based on who they like, or based on whose position they are trying to protect? I think.

I ask someone I have gotten to know and trust if I am being paranoid.

"No, you are not being paranoid at all," she says.

You want to think that the higher up you go in a sport, political stuff becomes less important and everything is more of a meritocracy. You want to believe that the best players make the U.S. Women's National Team, and that the best of those are the starters.

I am finding out that this is not necessarily the case. U.S. Soccer is a superb organization and, in Sunil Gulati, has a president who is a man of character and vision, but unfortunately, these advantages don't take politics or personal agendas completely out of the equation. So much of it comes down to where you went to school, what coaches are behind you, who is pushing you behind the scenes, and who your allies are among the veteran players. It also comes down to whether you are among the anointed ones, as decided by the U.S. developmental people. If they've "discovered" you and nurtured you and decreed that you will be the face of the team going forward, you are assured of having the soccer equivalent of the red carpet rolled out for you. You are a player the honchos want to succeed because they will not look good if you don't.

If you are someone who has come up outside the developmental infrastructure, on the other hand, you are in for a long, hard climb. You are going to constantly have to prove yourself. Tiffeny Milbrett and Shannon MacMillan, two former standout forwards for the national team, can tell you about that.

So can I.

It's a completely different path if you are a player such as Aly Wagner.

Aly, for a long time, has been the up-and-coming star of U.S. Soccer, everybody's favorite attacking midfielder. She was in a national camp, rooming with Mia Hamm, before she even got out of high school, and she earned her first cap at eighteen. She was the Gatorade High School Player of the Year and led Jerry Smith's Santa Clara team to the NCAA title in 2001, scoring seventeen goals and picking up eighteen assists and winning *Soccer America*'s Female Player of the Year honors.

A highly technical and creative player, Aly isn't necessarily the greatest pure athlete, but she can pass with anybody and is one of the top playmakers of her time. Sometimes Aly and I play together, but mostly she is the player I know I have to try to beat out if I want to get into the lineup. I'm not saying at all that Aly hasn't earned her spot; she's a gifted player (and will go on to have a fine ten-year run with the team). All I'm saying is that we are not always viewed through the same lens. If Aly loses the ball or doesn't execute a pass well, it's an aberration and is typically overlooked. If I commit the same mistake, it's a big fat strike against me and usually results in me getting pulled out of the game. The burden of proof is on me if I want to change the pecking order. For a long time, I resent that. I feel slighted and unappreciated.

With James's help, I start to use it as motivation.

You don't think I am good enough? You don't think I'm the player who should be your starter at attacking mid? I will show you.

It is not the first time that an industrial-sized chip on my shoulder works to my advantage.

Whatever politics and preconceptions may be in play around the team, I decide that I don't want to have any part in such nonsense. I have no hidden agendas. I want to play my best, and I want to win. It's that simple. Marci is the same way. There isn't any duplicity or drama about her. She is a soccer player, a darn good one.

"Greg brought me in because he needed a few more ball-winners," Marci says. "I knew that. I wasn't one of the main players on the team. I just wanted to help us win a World Cup."

I wish Marci could be my teammate forever, but I know that won't be the case. Indeed, not long after the World Cup, she departs the national team to take a position as the coach of Northern Illinois University.

My other new friend is Michele Gould, our physical therapist on the trip to China. On the second practice of the trip, I block a blast of a shot by teammate Lori Chalupny, the force of it jerking my foot outward and resulting in the worst sprained ankle I've ever had. Michele has me in ice buckets four or five times a day. When my foot isn't in the bucket, Michele puts it in a compression wrap or is massaging it to stimulate blood flow and healing. Michele is a savior. If she weren't with us, I don't think I would have even gotten on the field.

It's not a serious injury by any means, but the experience is a timely reminder of the importance of taking care of your body. The strength and vitality of your body are where it all starts. You need to listen to it and let it heal when it needs to heal. The injury is also a reminder of how invisible you become when you are not playing. Watching practice, I feel as useful as a deflated ball. The week that I am out, Greg pays no attention to me, and why would he? I am not playing. I am not out there training and helping the team get better.

When I am finally back on the field, I come off after a training session.

"How's your ankle?" Greg asks.

"It feels good. I'm ready to go," I say.

"Well, you don't look good," he says.

His comment really ticks me off, and I walk away. I've worked my tail off to get back and all he can tell me is I don't look good? I know I am doing myself no favors with this reaction. I am still immature, headstrong. My default response to a coach who is riding me this hard is to pull away and shut him out. Being coachable is one of the things I am still trying to learn.

I come off the bench in the first game, a scoreless tie against Germany, and I don't play well. I lose the ball a few times and try to force things too much. In our second game, against England, Marci gets banged up, and I come on for her and play much better, but then Greg and I have words after he yells something on the field and thinks I am disregarding him. Afterwards, Greg and I have a clear-the-air session. Bret Hall, Greg's top assistant, is there in case we need a mediator.

Greg tells me I am not coachable at times, and he needs to know I will hear him out and abide by his wishes.

I tell him that I feel that I can't do anything right and I am trying so hard to please him that it's taking away the fun of playing for me.

The conversation doesn't airbrush away the problems, but at least we've had a civil and honest dialogue and know how we both feel. After we return to the States, we have a residency camp in February, and Greg has individual meetings with us and asks us about our goals. I tell him about wanting to master free kicks, to be more and more of an offensive force, and to do everything I can to continue to improve as a player.

"My long-term goal is to be World Player of the Year," I say.

Greg chuckles, trying to stifle an all-out laugh when he hears this coming from the mouth of a twenty-four-year-old who hasn't even established herself in the starting lineup yet. I know it must sound incredibly audacious and arrogant, but I don't care. It's the truth. This is what James and I have talked about from the beginning.

It is what I've been visualizing almost from the first day on Ark Road.

"You must be able to see it happening in your mind before it can happen on the field," James said to me then, as he's done many times since.

The mind is like a brush-cutter in the woods, a bulldozer for your dreams, he says. It clears away the bramble and thicket so you have a path to follow. The mind sets out the path, and then the training enables you to follow it. "With a strong mind, you can become whatever you want to become," James says.

This is our plan, and I am sticking with it.

We head to Portugal for the Algarve Cup, where we open up against China. It's a 1–1 game late in the first half when Abby Wambach crosses the ball from the right, through the penalty area toward the left corner, where Stephanie Lopez runs the ball down. Stephanie nutmegs her defender and then toe-pokes a pass back to me. I juke a defender and crack a right-footed shot from twenty-five yards out into the upper left corner.

It turns out to be the game-winner and sets me on my way as we win all four games and I score in every one of them. I am named tournament MVP and Top Goal Scorer, and it is easily the high point of my young career. My confidence is soaring as we ramp up our preparation for the World Cup.

Maybe this will be a turning point in my career and in my relationship with Greg, I think.

Usually the more time you spend around a person, the better you get to know them. With Greg, the more time I spend around him, the more confused I become. I never know if he's going to tell me that I am on my way to being a world-class midfielder or that I am an embarrassment who is lucky to have a spot on his roster.

None of us have any luck reading him. When we come out for practice, our running joke is, "Who is he going to crush today?" People on the team who knew him before he took over as head coach say that they've never seen him behave this way, that there has been a total personality transplant. The funny thing is, when Greg was April Heinrichs's assistant, we all loved him. He was the guy you wanted to run into in the hotel lobby, have a cup of coffee with. He was our pal. He moved over one seat, and everything changed.

After a closed-door scrimmage against Japan in San Jose, California, in late July, Greg is profoundly unhappy and wants us to know it. We are all sitting on the ground in front of him. He is standing over us with his barrel chest and massive calves, a stout, well-scrubbed fireplug who always looks as if he's just gotten out of the shower. Greg played professionally for the North American Soccer League and Major Indoor Soccer League; they are not top pro leagues by any means, but Greg was a rugged defender who grinded out a living. You have to respect that. Greg Ryan is nobody to mess with.

"All of you who were part of the 2004 Olympic team, sit over here," he says, pointing to a line on the field. "You guys — Chupa [Lori Chalupny], Leslie [Osborne], and Marci — you go over there," pointing in a different direction.

You can feel an explosion coming.

"These are people who will fight for each other and for me and do whatever it takes to win," he says, referring to the two groups. Then he looks at the rest of us — Hope Solo, Tina Ellertson, Nicole Barnhart, Natasha Kai, and me — and screams, "You are people who don't have heart and don't work hard and don't care about the team." (Greg exempts newcomers Stephanie Lopez and Marian Dalmy from his classifications.)

I am so stunned I don't know what to say. I have been criticized before, but this is at a different level. No heart? Don't care about the team? I don't want to talk about this with the other players singled out. I don't want to talk to anybody. When Greg is finally done, I grab my stuff and head straight for the bus. I am far from a perfect player. I know I have so much to learn. But for him to be in our faces, telling us that we have no heart and don't work hard and don't put the team first, well, that is not true and not fair. Yes, he's the coach and I'm the player, but that is still completely clueless. If it is a motivational ploy, it's even worse.

It doesn't motivate me. It depresses me. My coach has just dismembered me.

Greg Ryan is under a great deal of pressure, I understand that. His team is a heavy favorite to bring home the first World Cup since 1999, and if he doesn't deliver, it's on him. I know he wants to keep us humble and hungry. I just don't think constantly demeaning people is the way to achieve that.

Greg stays on my case for the rest of the summer, his criticisms focusing on my defense and my tendency to take risks and take people on. My head keeps spinning. James sends a series of texts and emails to keep me grounded, and Marci reinforces them. When she sees how upset I am one day, she texts me and says, "You need to keep believing in what you can do. Everyone thinks you are so damn good. . . . Something great is coming your way."

The words help, and my new, self-designed Nike cleats give me a little emotional pickup too. I have three different designs, the first female Nike athlete to design her own cleats for the World Cup. There's a red-white-and-blue pair for the first round; for the quarters and semis, I have a yellow pair with the Five Pillars of Universal Soccer Academy in the back. For the finals, I have an orange pair, which stands for all my supporters and loved ones. James's initials, JG, are on the tongue, and 143 is on the side for Brian, our private code for *I love you.*

I don't know whether my shoes and I are going to start, but I feel fit and strong and ready to go. My parents and Brian have made the trip, and even with the problems my parents and I have been having, I appreciate that they will be in China to support me. Brian is so loyal and kind; it's comforting to know he will be there for me. I am rooming with Marci again, so I'm happy about that. One of the first things I do when we settle into our room is watch a film clip given to me by Phil Wheddon, our goalkeeping coach. It's a personal highlight reel — Phil gives one to everybody — and it helps a lot with my mental imaging. I see myself ripping shots from distance, delivering crunching tackles, and threading through balls. Phil does a masterful job with the clip. I watch it often.

Greg has been the coach for eighteen months now, in which time we have not lost a single game in regulation time. We've won forty-five games and lost one, and yet to me we still don't seem settled and confident as a team, even with the leadership of Kristine Lilly, the goal-scoring prowess of Abby Wambach, and the emergence of Hope Solo as an elite goalkeeper. Ten days before the World Cup is to kick off against Korea in Chengdu, Greg gathers us together and announces that we're changing formation from a 4-2-4 to a 4-3-3, adding an extra player in midfield. He sounds excited about it and tells me it means I am back in the starting lineup. I am wondering if he is messing with me or if he really means it.

It turns out he means it.

The opener against Korea, the youngest team in the field, doesn't go the way we hope. It's a rainy, sloppy field, and the Koreans have the better of the play through most of the first half. I win a ball in midfield and get it to Lilly, who steers a pass on the right to Abby, who opens the scoring in the fiftieth minute, but then Abby knocks heads defending our goal a few minutes later, suffering a nasty gash that requires eleven stitches to close. Greg doesn't want to lose Abby so he opts not to sub, and Korea strikes twice when she's out, the first on a shot beyond the 18 that slips through Hope's hands. Heather O'Reilly ties the score with a surgical, one-touch strike off a loose ball into the upper right corner in the sixty-ninth minute, sparing us an unthinkable defeat.

I'm not happy with the tie, but I am happy with my performance. I defend and win fifty-fifty balls and help orchestrate things offensively.

"You grew a lot as a player in this game. That was an excellent first World Cup game," Greg says.

We win our second game 2–0 over Sweden on two more goals by Abby, but the truth is that we still don't look our best. We're playing ugly, direct football, Greg's preferred style — bypassing the midfield and launching long balls to Abby or Lilly and hoping for the best. Our defense is tight, and Hope throws a shutout, and though I get subbed out for Shannon Boxx, I believe I've turned in another creditable effort.

We leave Chengdu for Shanghai, where we grind out a 1–0 victory over Nigeria to advance out of our group. I start a third straight game, this time getting subbed for Leslie Osborne, and Greg seems to sense my frustration with the way we are not connecting passes or playing possession soccer.

"If you spend all your time trying to look pretty, you are going to end up with big problems the other way," Ryan tells the press after the game. He approaches me later and asks if we can talk.

"I just want to check in and see how you are doing," he says. "I know I've been tough on you the last two and a half years, and I am so proud of how you've come along. You are going to be the future of this team."

It is one second later, maybe two, that he informs me that I will not be starting in our first elimination game against England.

This makes it official: I will never understand this man.

As we get ready for the game Greg wants to build morale and quiet any rumblings of discontent about how we are playing.

"We're outplaying every team in this tournament and haven't given up a goal in 11 v. 11 play. Not one," he says, reminding us that Korea's two goals came with Abby off the field for ten minutes.

Then we players have our own meeting, and it becomes very clear how deep the frustration goes. Abby says we are focusing too much on defense and need to be more aggressive offensively, no matter what Greg says.

"I feel like I can't play-make or build up the attack because we're just sending long balls to the forward line," I say.

Just about everybody speaks up, and the unrest is as thick as the Chinese smog, even if you wouldn't know it watching the England game, which we blew open with three goals in twelve minutes early in the second half. I only play ten minutes and can't say that I understand why, but the mayhem is just beginning.

We've advanced to the semifinals against Brazil, a rising power in the sport with a collection of dazzlingly skilled players who play as if they were jazz musicians in cleats, riffing and improvising as they go. Brazil is led by Marta, a twenty-year-old superstar, and her teammates Cristiane and Formiga. (When you are a big soccer star in Brazil, no second name is necessary.) The Brazilians have scored thirteen goals in four games. We are the top-ranked team in the world, and even though there are many new faces on this team, we are considered a strong favorite to win it all.

It is the most anticipated match of the 2007 World Cup and becomes even more so when Greg Ryan does one more shocking about-face, replacing Hope with Briana Scurry in goal. After a shaky start against Korea, Hope had recorded three straight shutouts. She has been our starter for a couple of years. Bri is a legendary keeper, a former World Cup champion, and an Olympic champion, but it is unprecedented to make such a switch at this point in a World Cup. Greg's explanation is that Bri is a superior shot-stopper and has a brilliant track record against Brazil. Hope is fuming, crushed, and it gets even worse when she apparently learns that Lilly and Abby had lobbied for the goalkeeping change.

I don't get it, because I think Hope is the best keeper in the world, and I still don't get how the drama keeps seeping to the surface like so much toxic waste with this team. The biggest match of the tournament begins with an own-goal in the twentieth minute, when Leslie Osborne tries to clear a corner kick with a low header and winds up putting it past Bri into our goal. Bri hasn't played a game in three months and looks rusty, tentative. How could she not? Then Marta wins a ball in our end and attacks, cutting into the box and firing a low, left-footed shot toward the right post. Bri gets a hand on it, but her reaction isn't quite quick enough. It's 2–0, Brazil, and when Shannon Boxx gets sent off for a second yellow card — a completely phantom call on a play when she is the one who was fouled — we are looking at playing the second forty-five minutes down a man.

I come on in the second half for Stephanie Lopez, but we are mostly playing desperate, skill-less soccer. In the seventy-ninth minute, Marta schools us again, flicking a pass to herself, wheeling around Tina Ellertson, carving up Cat Whitehill with a cutback, and beating Bri on the near side. We wind up losing, 4–0. It is not just our first defeat in more than eighteen months. It's the worst Women's World Cup loss in U.S. history, and I'm still trying to figure out how things unraveled so fast when I hear that Hope has just ripped Greg and Bri in a post-match interview.

"It was the wrong decision," Hope says. "And I think anybody that knows anything about the game knows that. There's no doubt in my mind I would have made those saves. And the fact of the matter is, it's not 2004 anymore. It's not 2004. It's 2007, and I think you have to live in the present. And you can't live by big names. You can't live in the past. It doesn't matter what somebody did in an Olympic gold medal game three years ago. Now is what matters, and that's what I think."

Aaron Heifetz, our press officer, tried to stop Hope from talking to the press, but Hope ignored him. In less time than it takes Marta to make one of her spin moves, outrage sweeps through our team and Hope is an instant pariah, isolated at our team meal and barred from our third-place game against Norway. She isn't welcome in the medal ceremony to get the bronzes we don't want. She isn't even allowed to fly home with the team.

"You wouldn't believe what's going on. Everybody is freaking out," I tell James in a text.

James tells me the Hope saga is all over the media at home too.

Hope is summoned to a meeting with the veterans, and they let her have it for breaking ranks and criticizing a revered teammate. Hope apologizes, but it is not enough. They want her to pay for her breach, and then pay some more. Hope is my closest friend on the team. She was directing her tirade at Greg and it almost came out as a rant against Bri. Still, I think this full-bore freeze-out is taking things too far.

In men's sports, people criticize coaches and managers all the time, and sometimes call out teammates too, and it's not that huge a deal. Things get hot and then it goes away. Often the guy speaking out is even lauded for having the courage to tell the truth. When it happens in women's sports, though, it always seems to be viewed as a nasty, claws-out catfight. I hate that our World Cup has devolved into this, but I am not going to be part of the Hate Hope Campaign. I am not going to abandon my friend. It's a gang mentality, and the gang wants to do everything but put Hope in stocks in downtown Shanghai.

It's too much. Hope was wrong, but this is even more wrong.

James and I talk it through and he agrees.

"Hope didn't kill anybody. She expressed an opinion," James says.

And what everybody forgets in their haste to bury Hope is that Briana Scurry once did pretty much the same thing — pointedly criticizing the person she had lost her job to, a goalkeeper named Siri Mullinix. Granted, Bri's comments came a couple of years later, not with the embers of defeat still hot and smoldering, but is there a statute of limitations on team loyalty?

Mullinix was the U.S. starter in the 2000 Olympics in Sydney, where the U.S. lost the gold medal game to Norway, 3–2, in large part because of some shaky goalkeeping. Bri, of course, had been the U.S. keeper for the 1999 World Cup champions, but in the long, happy aftermath had gotten out of shape and lost her job to Mullinix. Sometime before the next World Cup, Bri was asked whether she blamed herself for costing the U.S. the Olympic gold.

"I honestly believe that in my heart, yes. I knew I could've made a difference in that match," she said.

So I refuse to go along. I sit next to Hope. I talk to Hope. I've thought it through and I completely disagree with this calculated crusade to crush her, and I am not backing off that position.

This does not please the anti-Hope cabal at all.

"Be careful about who you align yourself with," somebody says. "It may come back to hurt you."

"I don't care. I am going to stand up for what I think is right," I tell them.

I do not play one minute against Norway in the third-place game. I sit on the end of the bench for virtually all of the three-game tour we do after the World Cup, watching Aly Wagner play attacking midfield. Do you think this is just one of those crazy coincidences in life? I don't.

It is the start of a long period of time in which I am viewed warily by some teammates and almost shunned by others. I am not happy about it. It's not as if I am going out of my way to be an outsider. But I'm not going to grovel to become part of the in-crowd either. I am an open book. I have my goals and my routine and a ton of extra work to do to get where I want to go. That is what drives me. Nothing is going to get in the way of that. I feel very misunderstood by my teammates and wish it weren't so. I don't want them to think I don't like them because I'm not going out with them all the time. There are probably ways in which I could do more to join in things without jeopardizing my goals. It's something I know I need to work on.

"At times I think Carli *was* perceived as not wanting to be part of the team," says Heather Mitts, my former teammate and fellow Universal Soccer Academy student who now broadcasts games for FOX Sports. "I was usually the organizer, and I would always try to get Carli to come out and do things, but she has this commitment and professionalism that was her complete focus at all times. Carli is a typical Jersey girl in a lot of ways. She has a hard exterior, but inside she has a big heart. She holds the people who are close to her dear and doesn't forget her roots. It's almost as if she lives in this little bubble and nothing is going to get in her way."

We're in the high altitude of Albuquerque, days before our last game of the season, and I need to clear the air with Abby, one of the staunch members of the anti-Hope brigade. I reach out to her and ask if we can talk. We're in our hotel. She comes to my room. She sits down on the edge of the bed.

"Abby, I respect you as a player and a person," I say. "You've already had a huge impact on this team, and I know that will continue. I don't know what you are hearing about me after all the stuff with Hope, but I just want you to know that I don't want to get dragged into any crap and any drama. I just want to help this team win. I work my butt off, whether I am starting or not starting. I leave it all out there every time I am on the field. People may get the wrong idea about me sometimes because I don't go out and stay to myself, but being on this team is my dream, and all I want is to contribute how-ever I can to the success the team has had for a long time."

Abby listens quietly. She is a big presence, even when she is sitting in a hotel room. She seems to take in what I am saying, and I think she appreciates the spirit behind it.

Then Abby tells me that she has some things to say too.

"You may not like it, but I hope you will hear me out," she says.

I nod, but I can feel my guard spike like a schoolkid's temperature.

"This has nothing to do with the Hope situation," Abby begins. "You expressed your opinion, and that is fine. You are a really good player, but your spot on the team is in jeopardy. You are walking a fine line. You are actually kind of like Hope, because you have to win back the hearts of the team. People don't see you fitting in, chemis-try-wise. They see you not wanting to join in things, and just sitting in the corner texting all the time. They feel that you don't trust them, and they don't want you on the field because of that. You also didn't have a very good World Cup, so that adds more questions. You are turning into Hope, and you better be careful."

I am stunned by what I am hearing. Beyond stunned. I know I'm not one of the girls; that much I am clear on. But the other stuff . . . My job is in jeopardy? People don't trust me? They are thinking they don't want me on the team?

I tell Abby that it is hard to have trust right now, with all the stuff going around.

"I do everything I can to work hard, be the best, and not get caught up in the drama. What is so bad about that?"

As far as my World Cup, well, I don't agree, because Greg would've been happy to have no midfield at all. He wanted us to lock people up on defense and boot the ball upfield and hope Abby scored a goal. He wanted no part of pretty soccer, possession soccer, and said so him-self. I don't want to get into all of Greg's mood swings either, how hard it was to deal with being the future of the team one day and Alpo the next.

I don't get into all this with Abby, because I'm not there to deconstruct Greg's strategy or motivational techniques. I ask Abby if there is anything else.

"Whether we have the same coach or a new coach, you need to know your position is on shaky ground. I hope you can use the time off to look at your mistakes and reevaluate things and come back determined to make things work."

Abby is finally done talking. My insides are seized up like an engine that has run out of oil. Abby talks a lot and she lives the way she plays . . . all out, and in your face. She has been a supporter of mine. After I was MVP in the Algarve Cup, she was quoted as saying the tournament was going to change the direction of my career.

"I think we've got a lot more really amazing things to see from Carli Lloyd. I just hope I can be around long enough to see them."

I don't think Abby is being mean-spirited by telling me all this, but I do think that she loves to inject herself into the middle of things. She wants to be on the good side of the veterans — in this case Lilly, Kate Markgraf, and Scurry. They want to punish me for siding with Hope, and now Abby wants to do the same, so she lets me have it. I don't appreciate her acting as if she is part of the judge and jury that will decide my future. Yes, I respect Abby and what she brings on the field, but this is way out of bounds.

Abby departs and leaves a palpable pall in her wake. I stare out the window, trying to get my head around what just happened. My insides churn. I am freaking out, and that is probably understating it. I am terrified that my lifelong dream is in danger of being torpedoed by backroom bickering and backstabbing.

Do these players really have the power to run me off?

James and I have a long talk about it. I begin to get some clarity. I need to find out if any of this stuff is true — if I am indeed in a precarious position.

It's not going to change how I work or go about my training, but I still want to know.

I call Cheryl Bailey, the general manager of the U.S. Women's National Team, and ask to meet with Dan Flynn, the CEO of U.S. Soccer.

"You need to speak to Greg before you talk to anyone else," Cheryl says. "He's your immediate boss. That's how we have to start."

I agree. Cheryl has always been straight with me and a classy person to deal with. I call Greg in the hotel.

"Hey, Greg, this is Carli. I need to talk to you right away. It's important. Do you have a few minutes?"

"Sure, Carli," he says.

Greg and I have had so many ups and downs, and he's under so much pressure in the wake of the Brazil debacle, that I really don't know how he's going to react. I just go straight at it.

"Abby and I just met in my room, and she told me that my spot on the team is in jeopardy and that people don't trust me and don't want to play with me," I say. "Is this true?"

Greg's square face almost seems to freeze before my eyes. He looks genuinely shocked.

"Abby has no right or place telling you your spot is in jeopardy," Greg says. "I don't know where she is coming from, but all I can tell you is that if I am the coach of the team, you are going to be on it. If someone else is the coach of the team, you are going to be on it."

He tells me that if I ever need anything or want to meet with him again to please let him know.

"Thank you, Greg. I really appreciate that," I say. It says a lot about Greg's character that he would go out of his way to reassure me on all this, given our tumultuous history.

The next day we play poorly and tie Mexico 1–1 to end our year. U.S. Soccer announces after the game that Greg Ryan will not be returning. It is not a decision that surprises anyone. I believe a change has to be made but still feel for Greg, and I will always be thankful that he was there for me when I needed it.

We say our good-byes and head our separate ways. We finish 2007 with one loss in twenty-four games, but that loss is viewed as a complete disaster and costs the coach his job, which gives you an idea of the expectations we face. I don't want to think about the World Cup or the Brazil game or anything else. I just want to get home and see

Brian and get back to Ark Road and the Blue Barn and train with James again. Everything else may be in chaos, but this is the one constant — I train with James Galanis, I get better, stronger, fitter. It has been happening for going on four years, and it's not going to change. It is foolproof. Having something in my life that feels foolproof is very comforting about now.

8

Olympian and Outcast

THE BEST PART ABOUT THE END OF 2007 is that it leads to 2008. There won't be another World Cup until 2011, of course, but at least we have the next best thing to look forward to — an opportunity to win our third Olympic gold medal in the last twelve years. We will go after it under the direction of a new coach, Pia Sundhage, a former star of the Swedish national team who sings Bob Dylan's "The Times They Are a-Changin'" at our first meeting and talks about a whole new style of play.

She wants us to dictate tempo, be brave and take risks, and possess the ball. Talk about music to my ears.

"Let's raise the level of attack in women's soccer," Pia says.

I love playing for Pia. I am finding new gears in training because her practices are so fun and challenging. Pia not only doesn't want to bypass the midfield, she wants everything to flow through it. She has made it clear that she wants me to become a focal point, and I am learning so much from her, especially about making runs off the ball and becoming more of a threat that way.

"You have all the tools to become the best player in the world," Pia tells me.

Back for another Algarve Cup a year after I was named MVP, I experience the biggest change of all in the third of our four games, against Norway. I open with a strong game in a 4–0 victory over

China, getting a goal and an assist, and play okay against Italy in our second game, but I am not good against Norway. The Norwegians pack the middle and sit back on us and pressure our every possession, and I never find my rhythm. I am fighting a slight groin pull and don't feel confident. I give away the ball as if I'm handing out Easter eggs, particularly in the first half, but the amazing thing is that Pia doesn't get on me and doesn't pull me.

"I want you to learn to play through games like these," she says.

The second half is better, and we wind up winning, 4–0, and we go on to beat Denmark to take the tournament. I feel so fortunate finally to have a coach who seems to appreciate what I can bring.

Another huge positive is Jill Ellis, Pia's assistant coach and my former U-21 coach. I have felt a special connection with Jill from the start. She is an authentic person, and I trust her completely. When she tells me something, I know it's motivated only by her desire to make me a better player. She approaches me before a training session one day.

"When you are in the attacking third, you should keep doing what you are doing — taking people on, finding the right pass, getting yourself forward," Jill says. "You are an incredible weapon in that part of the field, but one area I think is important to concentrate on is your turnover-to-completion ratio in other parts of the field, when we are building up."

She goes on.

"A true, world-class center mid should have a pass completion percentage in the mid to high eighties. When I look at your technical skills, I am thinking, *This player is so good — that's where she should be, not in the fifties or sixties.* This is all about making smart decisions and being conscious of ball security in our half of the field, getting us from the goalkeeper to the opponent's half. When you lose the ball there, it can put us in a dangerous situation. So it's good to be thinking about ball retention and not being wasteful and making every possession count."

Pia is not into statistical analysis, but Jill is. During our training sessions, she keeps track of completion percentages, and when

I come off, she'll tell me, "Sixty percent," or "Seventy percent." It becomes almost a game within a game for us. I totally embrace the idea of taking greater care with every possession — learning when to take risks and when to keep it simple. As a young player, I wanted to make an impression and often tried too hard to make a highlight-film play. Sometimes it would work. Other times the ball would get taken away. Like a young writer who reaches for big vocabulary words and elaborate constructions instead of something simple and direct, I am learning that less is more.

I am learning lots of things this year, probably as much as I have in my soccer career. During our training sessions when I'm home, James is encouraging me to connect more with my teammates and take advantage of what he calls "the togetherness factor." I keep to myself by nature, but during all the craziness during the Greg Ryan era and the World Cup, I withdrew even more. Not being sure about where I fit in or what my future was only heightened my natural insecurities. Now things are different, and I need to respond accordingly. James and I agree that it's important for me to do less texting and more connecting, to ask questions and reach out to people more. I will be twenty-six by the time the Olympics come around. I am not the new kid anymore. It's quite clear that my spot on the team is not at all in jeopardy.

"Keep listening to the coaches and be supportive of all changes and subs they make," James writes to me in an email. "They fully support you, and you need to do the same. Your time has come to become a leader and lead this team into Olympic qualification and then lead them to Olympic gold."

Getting all this positive feedback makes me want to work even harder. I am grateful that I have never had any issues with complacency. I sometimes can be my own worst enemy with my perfectionism, but the other side is that I am never satisfied and never feel as though I've made it, so I keep working as if I am trying to make the team. I guess the pain from getting cut from South Jersey Select has stayed with me all these years.

I never want to feel that way again.

Returning home after the Algarve Cup, I take a few days off and then get right back into the Ark Road office. I do lots of ball work and drills with James and Ryan Finley, a fellow Universal Soccer Academy student and a U-18 national team player; we take turns serving crosses to each other. I work on finishing and taking free kicks. My routine includes regular ninety-minute runs, twelve 800-meter interval workouts, and punishing hill sprints in Laurel Acres Park. I also do lots of body-weight strength training, cranking out sets of push-ups and crunches, in addition to calf raises, squats, and work with resistance bands. Every time I go home my fitness goes to another level. It's as if I am a car just out of the shop, freshly tuned up, running leaner and stronger, more explosive off the line. Without Ark Road and James, none of this would be possible.

We've qualified for the Olympics and the opening ceremonies are not even two months away. I have started all fourteen games we've played under Pia, all of them victories. Things have never been better on the field, but the drama on Black Baron Drive in Delran doesn't want to let up.

James is coaching my brother's U-17 team with the Medford Strikers, and my father is the parent-manager. For years my father has regarded James as all but a soccer messiah, but as I become more independent and start to make my own decisions, my father begins to shift his viewpoint. My parents both think that James was behind my decision to leave Rich, even though that is 100 percent not true. Then the 2007 World Cup happened, and my parents think that James gave me terrible advice on the Hope matter and was responsible for me being an outcast on the team.

James recognizes that it's important to be part of the team, but he didn't want me to get caught up in funky team dynamics. When I was pulled out of the starting lineup and then didn't play at all in the third-place game, my parents were convinced that this was almost all James's fault and that he was imperiling my career.

Things with my parents have never fully recovered from the Rich episode, and now every day I'm home it feels as if I'm tiptoeing through a minefield. I never know when someone is going to go off. I'm doing better than I ever have with the national team, but the discord at home weighs on me constantly. I make it a point not to spend too much time there when I am back on breaks. I stay with friends, or stay with Brian, and that becomes a point of contention too.

"I don't understand why you hardly ever have dinner with us and don't spend more time with your family after you've been away," my mother says.

The fact is that, even though I love my family, home is about the last place I want to be just now. I return to Jersey for a few weeks before I begin final preparations for my first Olympic Games. I do not need any family drama.

One night when I am out, I call home and my father answers. He starts right in on me. I don't want to hear it.

"You never want to hear it," he says. "You never want to hear anything we have to say. Why don't you get over here and get your stuff out of the house or I will throw it out the window?" I can't believe it has reached this point. But true to stubborn form, I don't back down.

"If that's how you want it, fine," I say.

I call Brian and tell him what happened. "I am going to get my stuff. Can you help me?"

Brian is shocked, but he is there for me, of course. He is always there.

I drive over to the house, pull up in front, and take a breath. I step over the curb I used to spend hours kicking the ball against. I look at the side yard that was my field when I wasn't down at the park. Being nostalgic is not my natural inclination, but it's inevitable given the circumstances.

I walk in the house and head straight upstairs. It's the saddest day of my life. I begin packing up all of my belongings. Brian arrives and has some suitcases to hold some more stuff. My mother and sister come into my room, and we all start crying. I am overwhelmed and so sad. I can't even believe this is happening.

When I'm finally finished, it is almost midnight. I head to Brian's mom's house, weeping as I drive. It feels so final, so crushing. I've lived my whole life in that house. Every minute of it. And now my own family doesn't want me anymore. Brian comforts me as only he can. I am so grateful for his support. I stay with him at his mom's house. I am exhausted and utterly drained. It takes a long time to fall asleep.

Days after I move out, I fly to South Korea with my teammates. The tournament is called the Peace Cup, and peace sounds very nice around now. I am rooming with Shannon Boxx, and it's fun, the attacking and holding mids bonding between training sessions and ice baths. Maybe I shouldn't be surprised given the events at home, but my body feels tapped out and my legs feel as if I'm wearing ankle weights. Our first game in the Peace Cup is against Australia, and I am brutal. It's my worst game since we played Norway in the Algarve Cup. I give up the ball often and beat myself up each time I do.

Our next game is against Brazil, and I'm in a much better place mentally. I've forgotten about Australia and am treating this as a clean sheet — except that ten minutes in I go up for a header and smack my nose into the back of somebody's head.

Blood starts gushing. I don't realize until the trainer and doctor come on the field that my nose is broken, pushed to the side of my face. I get subbed out, and they take me into the locker room, where the doctor examines me and with no warning snaps my nose back into place.

The pain is way worse than when I smashed into the Brazilian head.

I get fitted with a hideous mask with a beak that sticks out about two inches and makes me look like a falcon. Which is what we call the mask: the Falcon. I decorate it with a U.S. Soccer sticker and a Nike swoosh, but the artwork doesn't make it any less clunky.

We beat Brazil, 1–0, and I return the next game with the Falcon strapped on my face. I can't stand it. I play okay in a 2–0 victory over Italy, getting an assist on a corner kick, but in our final game against Canada, much stronger competition, I am not very good again. My passes are off and my touches are off, and I am not running the way I typically do, my frustration getting the best of me. Pia subs me out at halftime. It is the right move to make.

Afterwards, she talks to me.

"How can we handle this if this happens at the Olympics? I don't want to have to take you out. I want you to play every minute of every game. What do you think was going on tonight?"

"I think I just let the mask get in my head," I say. "I hate it. It's hard for me to see the ball and have clean touches. I wasn't playing well, and then I got down on myself when I made mistakes."

I don't tell Pia this, but this penchant for self-criticism is still one of my biggest challenges as a player . . . giving myself permission to screw up and not let it put me into a downward spiral. James talks to me about it all the time. We have more work to do.

The best thing about the whole trip is the connection I forge with Boxxy. Even though we've played together for several years, this is the most time we've spent together. We butted heads somewhat when I first came on the team, but now we're in a completely different place. She's such a committed, team-first player, doing tremendous work without a lot of fanfare. When you are on a team, at any level, you know who the people are who do the dirty work, who just keep putting out and giving, usually without much acclaim attached. That's Shannon Boxx. She centers me and supports me through all my struggles on this trip, and I am so thankful she is my roommate.

After a brief return home, we have a quick two games in Norway and Sweden. We crush Norway, 4–0, and beat Sweden, 1–0, and I have ditched the Falcon in favor of a new custom mask that is far more streamlined and manageable. I can actually play with it. I score in both matches and am back on my game, especially against Sweden.

Now there are only two games left before we leave for China and the Olympics—both against Brazil. We're 19-0-1 under Pia and an entirely different team than the one that showed up in that disastrous World Cup semifinal nine months earlier. We beat Brazil, 1–0, in Commerce City, Colorado, and head west to San Diego. Our fi-

nal game before the Olympics is on my twenty-sixth birthday—
July 16.

Just over thirty minutes in, I see Abby sprinting hard toward the
penalty box. I don't know what just happened, but Abby is ticked off.
I can tell just by how she's running. We have a saying on our team:
"Abby is seeing red." When Abby sees red, you better watch out. She's
coming after you, and coming hard.

The ball is loose and bouncing near the top of the box and Abby is
gunning for it, and so is a Brazilian defender named Andreia Rosa.
They collide violently. Abby goes down.

She goes down hard.

Oh no, I am thinking. *Abby, please get up.*

Abby does not get up. She motions for medical attention.

This is bad, I am thinking.

Unfortunately, I am not wrong. Abby Wambach, our leading scorer
for the year with thirteen goals and ten assists, a player who is on her
way to being the most prolific scorer in U.S. Soccer history, has broken her leg in two places. When the trainers ask if she can move her
leg, she says, "It's broken." She is gone for twelve weeks, gone for the
Olympics.

It is a grotesque sight, and it is unthinkable. This is Abby. She is
as close to indestructible as any athlete I know. The Olympics are
twenty days away.

Can this really be happening?

It is a horrific, sickening reminder of how fragile our world is. One
minute you are one of the top goal-scorers on earth, and the next you
are a hospital case.

There is a record crowd of more than 7,500 in Torero Stadium,
and almost all of its members are quiet. They celebrate in the eighty-
fifth minute, when Natasha Kai heads in my free kick for the only
goal of the game, but who is kidding whom?

We just lost Abby Wambach three weeks before the Olympics.
There is nothing at all to celebrate.

"Abby is a great player," Pia tells the press, "but it's not about one player, it's about the team. Still, we will miss her — Abby is Abby. We'll have to change a little bit."

Hope Solo, firmly entrenched once more in goal, insists there is too much character on our team for us to quit now and says, "We're a winning team, and we're going to find a way to win."

Abby says, "Above everything else, I'm only one player, and you can never win a championship with just one player. I have the utmost confidence in this team bringing home the gold."

The memory of our painful and awkward conversation at the end of the World Cup is long gone. A great athlete and teammate is badly injured. I watch her getting carted off the field, and all I feel is deep compassion for the great Abby Wambach.

9

Fine China

OUR BRAVE FACE about Life Without Abby lasts three minutes into our first Olympic game. We are playing Norway, a team we've outscored 12–1 in our last three meetings, in the coastal town of Qinhuangdao, about 200 miles east of Beijing. It is a summer resort area noted for its invigorating breezes and prime bird-watching opportunities. In the second minute, there is not a bird in sight. Only a ball in the back of the U.S. goal. Hope comes off her line, and leaping to punch out a long ball, she collides violently with Lori Chalupny. Both of them are sent sprawling. A Norwegian winger named Leni Kaurin takes advantage of the miscommunication and heads the ball into the vacated net.

Wait. It gets worse.

In the third minute, defender Kate Markgraf knocks a backpass toward Christie Pearce Rampone (she got married), but it is too soft, too slow. Before Rampone gets near it, Norway's Melissa Wiik swoops in and tucks the ball just inside the left post.

We aren't 180 seconds into the Olympics and we are down two goals. I'd expect the Great Wall to crumble before I'd expect us to open our Games this way. We never recover and lose 2–0. Norway is the only team other than the U.S. to win Olympic gold — the Norwegians won in Sydney in 2000 — so it's not as if they can't play. But come on, how can this be happening?

It is the first time the U.S. has ever lost in group play in the Olympics. Already the media is sounding the refrain that we can't win without Abby. I am not quite sure how the Olympic setup works, but I think our medal hopes might already be history until Pia explains that we can still advance to the elimination round if we win our next two games. Later that night, Pia asks Christie, Boxxy, and me to come see her in her hotel room.

"You are the core of this team," she says. "You are the ones who have to help us regroup and get the team going. We need a quick attitude change. We can't do anything about Norway. We've got a tough game against Japan in three days, and everything from here on has to be positive. I believe in this team as much as ever, but you are the ones who have to set the tone on the field."

It is a great meeting, and a pivotal message.

Japan is a technically skilled team, a side that likes to carve you up with a tiki-taka possession game. We are not at our best still, but we battle hard and play with commitment and urgency. In the twenty-seventh minute of the first half, our defender, Stephanie Cox, controls the ball near the Japanese end line, gets some space, and sends a cross toward the 18-yard line. I see what's coming and run onto it and belt a volley that dives just below the crossbar into the Japanese goal. It feels as if we've finally joined the Olympic party.

Our next stop is in Shenyang, a 2,000-year-old city in northeast China, not that far from Inner Mongolia. Our opponent is New Zealand, and a victory could lock up our group for us, provided that the Norwegians lose to Japan. We deliver a powerful, high-energy performance, winning 4–0 and advancing to the quarterfinals against Canada, thanks to the Japanese, who cooperate by beating Norway.

The Canadians have beaten us in only three of our forty-three matches, but the gap is narrowing. We won a hard-fought 1–0 game in our most recent meeting in the South Korea Peace Cup, and with Christine Sinclair, one of the world's premier goal-scorers, on their side, there isn't anybody thinking this game will be easy when it kicks off in Shanghai.

Angela Hucles scores to give us the lead in the first half, and then it starts to pour and lightning bolts begin flashing all around the stadium, as if the whole sky is plugged in. Play is stopped for ninety minutes, and we return to the locker room to wait it out. Some people stretch, while others sing and still others play games. I am content to rest up and get geared up mentally for the rest of the game. The lightning finally stops and the game resumes, and Sinclair ties it up with a missile just beyond a diving Hope's reach. A taut game heads into overtime, when finally, eleven minutes in, forward Natasha Kai converts a diving header, Abby-style. Tasha is immediately swarmed under a soggy and wildly happy celebration spilling everywhere.

Into the semifinals we go, in Workers Stadium in Beijing, a half-century-old concrete oval in the northeast section of the city, a world apart from the gleaming, new-age venues in Olympic Park. Our opponent is Japan again, and its players are in a confident, attacking mindset from the start. Hope parries away a threat in the opening minute, before a defensive lapse leaves an unmarked player in front on a corner kick. Hope has no chance, and we are down 1-0. It stays that way until the closing minutes of the half, when Heather O'Reilly has one of her signature high-speed bursts down the right flank and crosses in front, where Hucles slots in a left-footer to tie the game.

Then, in the forty-fourth minute, Markgraf finds me with a good ball near the center line. I shield the defender, take two touches, and send it ahead to Amy Rodriguez, who quickly finds Lori Chalupny, who eludes a defender on the left, cuts in front, and fires a shot under heavy pressure into the upper left corner. Up a goal, we are on our way to a 4-2 victory and another shot at Brazil, the team that stomped on us right here in China eleven months ago.

The Brazilians advance with a shocking 4-1 rout of Germany in the other semifinal, a reversal of the World Cup final result. Now we have our own kind of reversal in mind, and nobody wants it more than Hope, who has made it back from exile. Not only is she no longer

Goalkeeper Non Grata, she is the person we're counting on to hold down the hottest team on earth.

Hope had started the whole mess with her comments about believing she would've made a difference in that earlier game. Now she's got the blank canvas she wants. Let's see if she can paint a masterpiece. No, it's not a World Cup final, but it's the next best thing. I prepare with a careful reading of James's latest email. For years he has emailed me before major competitions. His words aren't just sustenance; they are my motivational rocket fuel.

He begins:

Ms. Lloyd,

Wow, you are in the final of the Olympics. It's been an amazing run thus far. Over the last five games you have grown as a player more than I imagined. You have gone from a player who works hard but wastes energy to a player who works hard and saves the energy for the right moments. Your play in midfield has more than helped your team get to this point.

After a game-by-game evaluation of my performance during the Olympics, James closes with two final points:

Your Chance to be the Biggest

Keep your head up high. With a little more work and a little more concentration you can steal the show and wake the world to who you are. You need to focus on being steady and taking advantage of your chances. I know you will get chances and you need to make them count. Two goals or an MVP performance will set you up as a top-5 player in the world, just in time [to be] the top player at the next Olympics.

The Game

This game is big to the world of soccer. However, you need to go in and treat it like another game. That's what you do best. Work the hardest, concentrate the most and be ready for anything. Don't give up and let it all out (empty the tank). I really feel that you are going to win because you're a better TEAM. They are individuals.

*Teams always beat individuals. But if you don't win just make sure
the Brazilians feel like they went through a torture chamber to get
the win. Don't give it to them easy. Pressure the hell out of them and
fight them to the end. Right now the GOLD is in your hands. Only
the Brazilians can take it off you. If you let them.*

James Galanis

From the start, it's clear that Marta and Cristiane, the dynamic stars
of the Brazilian side, are bringing all they've got, and so is Hope Solo.
I've seen Hope play lots of great games. I've never seen her more confident or sharper than she is tonight, on a rain-slickened field and in
humidity that makes the air feel like oatmeal.

At her best, Marta is a magician in a canary-yellow shirt, making
the ball appear Velcro-ed to her foot, and so it is in this epic game.
In the seventy-second minute, she runs down a ball to the left of our
goal, somehow eludes Heather Mitts and Kate Markgraf, and blasts a
left-footed shot toward the near post from point-blank range. Hope
dives left but raises her right arm as she does, almost as if she were a
traffic cop, stopping traffic. The ball slams into her right arm and ric-
ochets away.

Marta, World Player of the Year about a hundred times, cannot believe it. She buries her face in her hands.

It's the save of the tournament, of the year — probably one of the
greatest saves in Olympic history. It gives us an incredible lift. All
game, Hope is snaring crosses in traffic, punching away threats. We
have our best chance in the ninetieth minute, when Amy Rodriguez
gets in behind the Brazilian defense with only Barbara, the Brazil
keeper, left to beat. Barbara charges out, and Amy tries to chip it over
her, but Barbara grabs it easily.

With all the back-and-forth chances, the drama keeps building,
and now the game goes into two fifteen-minute overtimes, Brazil
looking for its first major championship, the U.S. looking for its third
Olympic gold in four tries. All I can think as overtime begins is:

This is why I train. This is why I run those hills in Laurel Acres, do those 800 repeats, the ninety-minute distance runs. It's why I do all the body-weight exercises, why James and I keep pushing for more and better ways to get me fitter. I empty the tank in training, so the tank is never empty in games.

We are in Brazil's end, six minutes into overtime, when Lauren Cheney, who has come on for Lindsay Tarpley, slips a short pass to me. I hold off a defender and backheel a ball to Amy, who takes a touch and threads it back to me under heavy pressure. I see a sliver of space and explode forward, take a touch, and let fly with my left foot, the ball launching low and hard, a skidding one-hopper heading toward the right corner. Barbara dives to her left.

She might get a fingernail on the ball. She cannot stop it. The ball is in the Brazilian goal, and I am running toward my teammates, arms pumping, joy pouring from me as I hug Boxxy first and then everybody else. I run over and hug Pia. She is the one who believed in me, who has started me every game this whole year, who wants me to be the hub of the U.S. attack.

There are still twenty-four minutes to play, and Brazil keeps the pressure on. Marta does a pullback move, spins left, and rips a shot just over the crossbar. The pressure on the defense and Hope is constant. In a counterattack in the final minutes, I get behind the defense and spank another left-footer, this one thudding off the far post. Brazil still has life. The clock is crawling; every second feels like ten seconds. Brazil has three straight corners at the end of the game. Marta's inswinging ball finds Renata Costa near the far post, but her header hits the outside of the netting. On the final chance, Costa arches a ball in the box to Cristiane, who drives a low header that Hope stops. The whistle blows. We are jumping, screaming, crying, embracing. Nobody thought we could ever win without Abby, and now we've done it.

Hope runs out of the goal and wraps me in her arms, and neither of us has to say a word about the sweetness of this ending — Cup outcasts turned Olympic heroes. We are a team again, all in it together, fighting for each other, sacrificing for each other, with lots of perseverance and perspiration, not drama or dissent. It is a total team triumph, from Angela Hucles, our leading scorer up top, to Heather Mitts and the rest of our relentless defenders in the back, to Hope's all-world effort in the net. You can't single anybody out. We've all given everything we've got, for 120 minutes, the contributions coming from everywhere. If Lauren Cheney doesn't slip me a deft pass with the outside of her foot seconds before the game-winner, if Amy Rodriguez doesn't hold off two defenders and find me on a give-and-go, there is no gold medal–winning goal. That's the beauty of soccer: so many little moves have to be made, so many little battles have to be won, to produce the ultimate victory. Our joy, a feeling that is as pure and good as the gold medal itself, is well earned and shared by everyone.

Later that night our team liaison in Beijing, a young Chinese woman whose nickname is Bean Bean, takes us to a private party. David Beckham is there, and I get to talk to him. The actor Vince Vaughn is there too. I get a photo with both of them. My gold medal is around my neck. It stays there for a long time.

A week after I return home, a parade is held in Delran in my honor, complete with the high school marching band, the Knights of Columbus, the VFW, and most every fire truck, police car, and EMS vehicle in town, along with hundreds of little kids in their soccer uniforms. My old coaches, Joe Dadura from the Strikers, Rudi Klobach from Delran High, and Glenn Crooks from Rutgers, are there too. It is Labor Day. The parade starts at Vermes Field, where I used to play, and heads down Tenby Chase Road to Conrow Road to the high school. I ride in the top of a fire truck, wearing a black dress and a gold medal, and wave until my arm hurts. My parents are also waving, in the back of a red convertible. The day winds up with a ceremony on the football field, where a bunch of politicians give speeches and everybody talks about me, and my parents and brother and sister are all sitting on the stage, a penalty kick away from Brian and me.

I don't tell anybody about getting booted out of my own house right before the Olympics. It would kind of spoil the moment.

From start to finish, the event is a sweet, small-town tribute, and I appreciate the sentiment and the chance to share the Olympic achievement with so many people who have been there for me along the way. But the truth is that I don't like being fussed over, and never have. I'm way more comfortable practicing volleys on Ark Road than listening to people celebrate me and tell me how great I am. I never want to be rude to anyone, but I am a person who likes her inner circle small and her gatherings intimate. I try to explain this to my parents when they begin to plan a post-parade party at the house.

"I know you want to include a lot of people and make it a big celebration, but I'd really prefer to have it just be close family and friends, since I don't see them very often," I tell my mother.

"Carli, so many people have shared in this and want to be a part of it. We can't not include them," my mother says.

I don't want to start more dramas, so I don't carry it much further.

More than anything I want the strife to go away and to be able to enjoy this time with my parents, brother, and sister. This is not how I want to go through my life, exiled from my own flesh and blood, people I love and have spent my whole life with.

Things seem to be improving a bit as the fall arrives. I sort of move back in, staying at home occasionally, but the friction is always quick to flare back up.

I realize I need to be out of the house for good and start looking for a place to buy, and ultimately find a nice townhome with a fireplace and clean, airy feel about it. I make a couple of trips back to my parents' house to collect a few last items.

Three months after the exhilarating run at the Olympics, it's clear to me that my relationship with my parents is at an all-time low. I spend the first Thanksgiving of my life away from them. I am with Brian and his family, and I love them, but I still have so much sadness. As Christmas approaches I email my parents because I need some photos of me when I was young and they have my photo albums. I tell them they can leave them on the porch and I will pick them up. Nobody is home when I arrive. I walk up to the porch and see several big boxes of my things. My father has packed up my stuff and left it for me. In one of the boxes are the scrapbooks and bind-ers he meticulously kept from the very beginning of my soccer career. Newspapers clippings, press releases, tournament results, awards.

Everything.

Next to the bags is a card and my Christmas gift, a set of pots and pans for my new home. I drop off my gift for them — a gift certificate to Cheesecake Factory — and lug the boxes to my car. I leave the pots and pans behind.

10

Letting Go of Gold

JAMES IS CONCERNED ABOUT ME, probably more con-
cerned than he has been in almost five years of working together. It's
not so much the family drama as the way I look in training at the end
of 2008 and early in 2009. I am putting in the time, training hard.
But James doesn't see the same intensity, the I'll-prove-them-wrong
edge that has driven me for so long.

"You are not training at full capacity. You're not as mentally engaged as you need to be," James says. "You've got to train harder and
be fully committed mentally."

I get a little defensive. It hasn't happened often in my time with
James, but he has never questioned my commitment before.

Not once.

"What do you mean, train harder? I'm here. I'm doing the work. I
don't think I'm slacking off."

More than anyone I've ever met, James Galanis finds a way to be
supportive and a hard-ass all at once. There have been times he criticized me pointedly and somehow I still felt as if I'd gotten a hug. That
is not easy to pull off.

"You are doing the work, Carli, yes," James says. "But it's not the
same way as you've always trained. I am watching closely, and I see a
difference. I need you to get back to being the underdog."

I wish I could say he is wrong, but he's not. James knows exactly what the issue is, and so do I. It's the Beijing afterglow. Suddenly, for the first time since I've been on the national team, I am the flavor-of-the-day for the media, getting attention that usually goes to Abby or Hope or Aly Wagner, that went to Mia Hamm and Julie Foudy and Kristine Lilly before that. I am named U.S. Soccer's Player of the Year. I don't think it goes to my head. I don't want it to go to my head. But when you're being celebrated as never before, it's natural to stop and think, *I guess I* am *pretty good.* James goes right after it, treating these nascent, complacent thoughts as if they were a pack of termites ready to chew through the foundation we've worked so hard to build. He is happy to play the role of exterminator. He begins by scribbling a message on a little chalkboard in his basement, where I do off-season strength and fitness training.

The sign reads:

THE OLYMPICS ARE FORGOTTEN

James does everything but brand the words into my brain. It's good that he does.

Things are a struggle for me from the outset of 2009. I am on fire in our first camp of the year in January, feeling fit and playing in top form, certain that I've put the afterglow issue behind me, but I lose my sharpness as camp goes on. Pia notices, of course.

"I don't want you to lose your drive to be the best," she says. "You have to stay switched on through every single training session."

"I know you're right," I say. "I haven't felt challenged. I've been kind of bored. I know I have to step it up."

Camp finishes on a much better note, but there are a number of new players in the mix, especially in the midfield, and we don't play our best in our annual visit to Portugal for the Algarve Cup, falling to Sweden on PKs in the final. Abby is still not quite back from her broken leg from the previous summer, and with another World Cup still two years away, it's a low-key year for the national team, so my main focus is on my new team, the Chicago Red Stars, of Women's Professional Soccer (WPS). I am one of the marquee players on the team, along with Lindsay Tarpley, Brazil's Cristiane, and Megan Rapinoe, but it turns into a season-long nightmare, as we never really mesh.

After winning only one of our first nine games, we never fully recover. I wind up playing a good deal of forward, but score just two goals in twenty games and feel out of my element almost the whole season. We finish 5-10-5 and don't make the playoffs. I book out of Chicago in early August and head for the Jersey Shore, where I hang at my aunt Patti's house and reconnect with Brian.

After a few days off, I get back to training with James. It's just what I need to put a frustrating season behind me. I have started to make big changes in my diet, cutting out candy and sugar and almost all carbs, and I feel leaner and better already. It's all good, until my phone rings one day. I am at home in my bedroom. I've just finished a monster workout with James. The caller is Pia Sundhage.

"Carli, I want to give you a heads-up before the official email goes out," she says. "You don't have a renewed contract [with U.S. Soccer] for 2009." (Twice a year we either get renewed, not renewed, or bumped down a tier.) "If you do get a contract, it may not be Tier I [the top pay scale]."

I am stunned. I know I didn't have a great season in Chicago, but not to be renewed by a coach who told me she thought I could be one of the best players in the world?

I am on the verge of a meltdown but try not to give that away.

"Okay. Can I ask why?"

"Well, you weren't in your best form early in the year, and then the WPS season didn't go the way you or I were figuring it would either. The consensus is that, for whatever reason, you are not the same impact player you were.

"Now, what happens from here is up to you. You will have plenty of chances in September, October, and December to show that you have improved your game and get your contract, but I wanted to let you know."

I hang up the phone and think I am going to throw up. I am livid. I am sick. It feels as if my world is crashing all around me, my brain stuck on a nasty and self-critical refrain:

How could I have screwed this up? How could this be happening? A year ago I became a gold medal hero and the Player of the Year and

now U.S. Soccer doesn't want to renew my contract. Can anybody tell
me how it has gotten to this point?

As angry as I am, as much as I might want to blame somebody or
beat myself up, I know this is no time for self-pity. It is time to go to
work as I never have before.

Without delay, James and I launch into two-a-day sessions, determined to pound me into the greatest shape I have ever been in. I run
distance. Run sprints. Run hills and run-through drills. I am sore
and miserable and exhausted, mentally and physically, as I push beyond thresholds I've never crossed before, but the hurt is accompanied by empowerment.

I am in the best condition of my life. I don't think it. I know it. Between the workouts and my dietary changes, my confidence picks up,
and even though I am anxious about the upcoming camp, I also am
hell-bent on kicking butt and showing Pia how wrong it was not to
renew me.

The underdog is back in a big way.

Before I leave for camp, James emails to say how fit I am and how
proud he is that I did all the work without complaining.

"You are going to not only get a contract but also take over the
WNT," he says. "Don't worry. Just keep working. We are all in. No
other way."

Camp starts at the training center in Carson, California, on September 21 and goes for twelve days. From the time I step on the field
I am as sharp and confident as I've been in months. My mind is completely clear, unburdened by doubt or complication. One thing that
happened after the Olympics, subconsciously I think, is that I felt I
had to meet all these expectations people had — that I had to make
magic happen on each possession. So instead of playing simply, naturally, I would sometimes force things and take needless risks. Nothing can mess you up on a soccer field more than that.

Now I am free of that, and the difference is striking. Pia comes up
to me after day two of camp.

"You are looking very fit, very good," she says. "It's good to see you
back in top form."

"I don't want to go backwards again," I say. "I'm hitting the delete button on last season. It's a fresh start, and I feel like I'm ready to crush it."

A few days later, I am leaving breakfast and I run into Pia again. She asks if we can talk.

"When I look at you now compared with the player I saw in the Algarve and in the WPS, the difference is truly night and day. How did this happen? It would help me to know how you did it."

"It's pretty simple, Pia. I got my ass kicked by my trainer for five weeks. I worked harder than I ever have in my life, so now I feel fit and confident, and I think that is what you are seeing." I remind her of what I've told Greg and Jill and other coaches I've worked with through the years: a high level of fitness doesn't come easily to me. Some players can do minimal training and go hard for ninety minutes. That is not me. When I do all the extra stuff that I need to do, it changes everything.

"Well, I am very happy for you," Pia says. "You've shown me so much, and you deserve your contract, so we will get that done."

I wind up getting traded to the Jersey team in WPS, Sky Blue FC, and that is more good news, because I get to be near home. There has been no thaw with my parents, but otherwise I am in a much better place than I was a few months ago. James doesn't tell me this at the time, but he thinks getting knocked on my can was exactly what I needed.

"Carli got a big contract in Chicago, the coach fussed over and told her, 'You are going to be my star, you are going to be my number 10 [playmaker],' and she fell for all that nonsense," James says. "I think she thought she could just coast through the WPS season. She played horribly, and it was a great investment because it taught her that it doesn't work to train at eighty or ninety percent. You can't take your foot off the gas, ever. It was the best possible lesson for Carli to learn."

It's the holiday season, and a Christmas cookie party sounds great to me. Aunt Patti has invited me down to her home in Wildwood Crest, near the southern tip of the Jersey Shore, for a bake-a-thon. It's a Saturday morning, and the weather is brutal, snow coming down hard. Aunt Patti's house is almost ninety miles away.

"I'm not so sure you should go," Brian says. "The roads look terrible. Just wait it out for a while and go later."

"I'll be fine," I say. "I'll take it easy. I've got four-wheel drive. The roads should be empty. I will take my time."

Brian tries to dissuade me, but I am in go mode. I want to bake cookies with my aunt and cousin Jaime.

"Just watch out for the black ice," Brian says. "The first thing you tend to do is grip the wheel tighter and slam on the brakes, and that's the worst thing you can do. Don't hit the brake if you fishtail. Just turn into the skid and get the car back under control."

"I'll be careful," I promise.

I jump in my black 2006 Nissan Pathfinder and off I go. I take back roads to the Garden State Parkway and head south. The plows have been through, and it's really not so bad. I'm cruising along, the roads are pretty clear, and I'm about twenty minutes away, driving in the left lane, which is the clearest. It's starting to snow harder, but everything is okay until out of nowhere I hit an ice patch and the car starts to skid to the left. I remember Brian's caution, but I don't remember soon enough. I tighten my grip on the wheel and hit the brake. Now I am skidding to the right, and I jerk the wheel in that direction, probably too hard, and soon the car is completely out of control, careening across two lanes, heading for a tree. I am powerless and my car is going where it's going. Time feels as if it has completely stopped. It is the scariest moment of my life. I wait for the horrible impact and the sickening sound and the end. My mind is a blur. I don't even have time to think of Brian and how much I love him and how sorry I am I didn't listen to him. I don't think about how my life and all my soccer dreams are going to end on the way to a cookie party on the Garden State Parkway.

It's almost as if I am in a trance.

I crash into the tree, and all the airbags blast out, but the car has turned enough that it's not head-on — my left front tire takes most of the impact. The tree slows me down, but my car is still hurtling forward, totally out of control, heading for tidal water. I have no idea how deep it is, but I do know Pathfinders do not float. The car plows through a small thicket of woods and plunges into the water, which starts pouring into the car, instantly, the fastest incoming tide I've ever seen. Now it's a race against the tide. I can't get out of the driver's side because of the damage and the air bags, so I hop over to the passenger's side. I look out to the right and the water looks deep. I muscle the door open and scramble up onto the roof of car, and just as I do I hear a man's voice.

It's a middle-aged guy with gray hair and a ruddy complexion. He must've been behind me and seen me skid off the road. He pulls over to see if he can help. I am still on the roof of my car.

"Are you okay?" he says. "I have something that can help."

He lays down a long piece of metal that almost looks like a ramp you'd use to roll lawn mowers onto a flatbed truck or something. He sets the ramp up so it's kind of a footbridge that will take me from my rear bumper to solid land. I climb down off the roof, put my foot on the bumper, and step onto the ramp. It works perfectly. I take a few steps and join my Good Samaritan on beautiful, hard ground.

"Thank you so much for stopping. I don't know what I would've done without you," I say.

"It's no problem," he says. "I saw the whole thing right in front of me. You are very, very lucky."

"I sure am," I tell him.

I stand on the edge of the marsh and look at my half-submerged Pathfinder, and only then do things start to compute in my brain. I have just skidded off a parkway, hit a tree, totaled my car, and landed in water, and I don't have a scratch on me. My neck will be sore for a couple of days, and I am plenty shaken up. But otherwise, I could play a full ninety minutes.

Yeah, lucky would be the word.

I call 911 and Brian, tell him what happened, and assure him that I am fine but that I am sick about my car. This is the first new car I've ever bought, earned with the money I made playing soccer, and it's sinking deeper every second.

"The important thing is that you are fine. You can get another car," Brian says.

Then I call my cousin Jaime and tell her what happened. Jaime and my uncle come and get me at mile marker number 14 on the Parkway. In the meantime, the police pull up, followed by an ambulance. The EMS workers ask me if I need medical assistance or need to go to the hospital.

"I'm fine. I'm really fine, thank you," I say.

I explain to the police how my car wound up in the water. I cross back over the metal ramp and grab a few things from the back of the car — probably not the smartest move, but what can I say? I like to take care of my stuff. The tow truck arrives and hauls my Pathfinder to the junkyard. I warm up in the back of the police car for a few minutes, and then Wayne and Jaime arrive, and we finally get back to their house by the Shore. I don't remember too much about the cookies.

Later, I joke to Aunt Patti that maybe we should forget the cookie party concept. A year earlier, my mother and sister were invited as part of an effort to patch things up, but there was a big blowout the first night and they wound up leaving at one in the morning. Another year somebody got sick and had to go to the hospital.

"It's The Curse of the Cookie Weekend," I tell Aunt Patti.

The 2010 season gets off to the best start. I stay off of ice, and we finish off a strong Algarve Cup with a 3–2 victory over Germany.

"That's the greatest game I've ever seen you play. You looked so fit, and you owned the middle of the field," Pia says.

After a miserable WPS season in Chicago in 2009, I can't wait to get going for Sky Blue. We split our first two games, and I'm not altogether thrilled with my performance, but about a third of the way through our third game — against my old team, the Red Stars — I feel I'm back in prime form. I'm playing holding mid because my teammate, Yael Averbuch, is out sick. I am tackling well, winning balls, changing the point of attack, and spraying the ball out wide. In the twenty-seventh minute, I play a ball to Natasha Kai, and as I do I lose my footing, all of my weight goes on my left leg, and my left ankle buckles like a cheap chair. I hear the crack. I lie on the field for a few moments and walk off on my own. I want to tape it up and go back in, but the trainer says the ankle doesn't look right and the team doctor believes it's broken. I go to the emergency room at halftime, and the X-rays confirm that I have a broken fibula.

I get a cast for two weeks, and then a boot. I start jogging at six weeks, at the team's urging. It is way too much, way too soon. It still hurts, and I have to back off until I attend the national team camp in July. Even then I am not right, and I mostly work out on the side. Finally, I start to train in late August and into September and get back on the field with the national team at the next training camp in late September. I make my first start for the U.S. since March on October 2 against China, and it seems as if it's been ten times that long. I am anxious about being back out there, but I play simply and effectively, keeping control of the ball and linking passes with the forwards, going for understatement rather than flash, and then we are off to Cancun, Mexico, for World Cup qualifying.

Before the games start, Pia meets with me and underscores how much the team needs me to step up, especially in the attacking third.

"You have all the tools in the world and can be the best, and that's what we need," she says.

"I know I can get more fit. That's what I want too," I say.

We breeze through games against Haiti and Guatemala — I am named Player of the Match in both — but then we look only so-so in a 4–0 victory over Costa Rica before we play the host team, Mexico, in the CONCACAF semifinals.

In front of 8,000 fans in a boisterous, sold-out stadium, we pick a horrible time for a letdown — giving up a goal in the opening minutes only makes the crowd that much louder. I tie it up, winning a scramble in front after a Megan Rapinoe cross, in the twenty-fifth minute, but the Mexicans answer right back with another score. We are totally out of sync, playing kickball, and even though we outshoot Mexico 10–1, in the second half the score does not change. I am angry and in complete disbelief at our collective level. Mexico took it to us, and we allowed our nerves to make us tentative and inconsistent, an effort that made U.S. Soccer history . . . the first loss to the Mexican women in twenty-six matches.

Now we are in a major fix. We have to beat Costa Rica for third place, and then beat Italy just to qualify for the World Cup. Everybody figured we'd waltz through qualifying. Maybe that was the problem. We have a team meeting, and I bring up the disastrous game against Norway to start the 2008 Olympics.

"We have to be more of a team. We can't just think that because it says USA on our jerseys teams are going to lie down for us," I say.

We are better in a 3–0 victory against Costa Rica, and then we head to Italy right before Thanksgiving for our biggest game since the 2008 Olympics.

Playing in the ancient northern Italian city of Padua, we generate tons of chances and are playing well, but not finishing. I am so fresh and energized that I feel as if I could run to Rome and back. I am all over the field. In extra time, I ping a long ball to Abby, who flicks it to Alex Morgan, a new kid with great speed and a knack for scoring big goals, and she finishes it. We win, 1–0, and head back to the States for a return match with Italy in Bridgeview, Illinois.

We have a series of meetings and a film breakdown, and before one of the meetings the team has a ceremony in honor of my 100th cap, a milestone I will reach in this next game. Paul Rogers, our goalkeeper coach, shows a video of me in action. Christie Pearce, our captain, gets up and addresses all of us.

"This is a great achievement and well deserved," Christie says. "Carli, I've seen you grow so much from your college days at Rutgers until now. Your dedication and hard work are unmatched, and mentally you are so strong. You are someone who never quits and never backs off, and that's how you've gotten to this point."

Everybody applauds. There is a slide show of pictures of me through the years, and a framed USWNT jersey with number 100 on it is presented to me. Later, I receive a Rolex from U.S. Soccer, which I upgrade with an engraving that says:

100TH CAP
ITALY
NOVEMBER 27, 2010

It is a happy day all around, even though we play a sloppy game, winning 1–0 on a goal by Amy Rodriguez. The only thing that matters is that we have qualified for the World Cup in Germany next summer and averted the unthinkable.

I stick around Chicago for a day to watch the Eagles lose to the Chicago Bears and then go into a six-week break with my ankle almost completely healed and my head in a good place. I can't wait to be back in my home and to not have to say good-bye to Brian for a while. Aunt Patti throws another cookie party, and miraculously, nothing bad happens. We just have fun together and bake into the night.

After giving my body a little time to recharge, I dive back into phase 2 of James's training, the goal being to further establish myself as a core player with the national team. The training begins with a series of long runs to build up my aerobic base, finishing with the prescribed ninety-minute runs. I run in the snow and cold, in whatever. I layer up and go. I mix in indoor training twice a week, and then I start up with track workouts, doing 800-meter repeats on some days and twenty-five sprints up the Laurel Acres hill on others.

To mix it up, I get in the car and drive twenty miles west, across the Walt Whitman Bridge, and into Philadelphia. I turn onto Benjamin Franklin Parkway and head toward the Philadelphia Museum of Art, home to the steps made famous by Sylvester Stallone/Rocky Balboa on the big screen. There are seventy-two steps in front of the museum. Sometimes I take them one at a time, other times two at a time. I have never stepped foot inside the museum, only on the concrete leading up to it. I run Rocky's steps thirty-five times. Nobody is playing "Getting Strong Now" in the background, but that is exactly what I am doing.

11

Empty Cup

JAMES GALANIS IS MY GREATEST SUPPORTER, but Pia Sundhage is not far behind. All year in the run-up to my second go at the World Cup, Pia tells me that she wants me in attack mode, wants me to be the focal point of everything. The day she announces our Cup roster — it includes twelve first-timers — Pia tells me that the whole key for us is going to be me getting forward as much as possible and Shannon Boxx taking care of things as the defensive midfielder.

I love Pia's faith in me; playing for her couldn't be any more different than life under Greg Ryan, who treated me as if I were radioactive at the end of the 2007 World Cup. It's just that sometimes my game to-do list seems overly ambitious. Pia wants me to be the playmaker, make runs behind the forward line, switch the point of attack, distribute the ball around the field, key our possession game, and tackle and win balls on the defensive end.

A month before the World Cup we have two games against Japan. Before the second one, in Cary, North Carolina, I speak to Pia after a training session when it seemed as if she thought I was wearing a cape with a big "S" on it. I am frustrated, and Pia can see it.

"What do you need from me?" she asks.

"I'm thinking too much out there about everything you want me to do," I reply. "I'm not playing freely, and it's affecting my confidence. I'm much better when I can just play."

Pia hears me, but I know that she is feeling enormous pressure. She's led us to Olympic gold, but this is the ultimate prize — what we've been working for ever since we crashed out against Brazil four years earlier.

This is why she was hired.

We're the number-one-ranked team in the world, but we've had our bumps along the way this year, for sure. After surviving the qualifying scare, we lost our first game of the year to Sweden and followed a stellar Algarve Cup with our first loss to England since the War of 1812. It was actually 1988, but that's still pretty ancient history. We seem much better for having gone through all that. We win the two games against Japan, then beat Mexico, 1–0, in our send-off game in New Jersey. Next, we fly to Salzburg, Austria, for our final training sessions before traveling to Dresden to play North Korea in our first group game. Brian, Aunt Patti, Uncle Wayne, and Jaime are there, as well as Jaime's husband Alex and his brother Andrej. Though I'm grateful for their love and support, I'm concerned that they could be a distraction if I'm worrying about their tickets and how they're doing. I do not want to be distracted. It happened four years ago in China, and we know how that played out.

I am nervous as the North Korea game begins, but I ease my way into it and get tons of work done, possessing the ball effectively and playing some nice balls, one of them a long, left-footed pass to Abby, who swings out to the left flank and crosses it in to Lauren Cheney, who heads it in for our first score of the tournament. Rachel Buehler drills home our second goal and we score a 2–0 triumph, then keep it going by knocking off Colombia, 3–0, a victory that is highlighted by a missile of a strike outside the box by Heather O'Reilly. Megan Rapinoe follows with a wonderful hustle play, throwing the ball in, sprinting toward the box, and finishing with a superb strike of her own. I get my first World Cup goal to wrap up the scoring. Then it's on to the city of Wolfsburg, where we play Sweden. We're assured of advancing out of our group, and all we need to do is tie Sweden to avoid a quarterfinal against Brazil.

Every tournament, and every year, has its own narrative, and this year's seems to be that we refuse to do things the easy way. Sweden is a physical team; they always play us tough, and with our coach being an iconic Swedish player, that goes double this time around. The Swedes convert an early PK and score a freakish second goal when a direct kick caroms off of Amy LePeilbet's thigh into the goal. We lose, 2–1, the first time the U.S. women have ever lost a group stage game. Sweden wins our group, and we get Brazil, as tough a quarterfinal as you could ever have, back in Dresden.

I am not terribly stressed about having to play the Brazilians, honestly. The way I see it, we owe them for what happened four years ago. They are staying in the same hotel as us, and it seems that wherever they go, their fans like to pound on drums and break into song, as if they were on the beach in Rio during Carnival. It's part of their culture, I understand that. But I don't have to like it.

I don't have to do anything to work up an edge about the Brazilians.

We score on an own goal off a superb cross by Boxxy in the second minute, and then the U.S. and Brazil go at it in a two-hour quarterfinal crucible, a game with little rhythm, lots of tension, and more twists and turns than an amusement park ride. In the sixty-fifth minute, Marta flicks the ball to herself, bores in on Hope, and gets blocked by Rachel Buehler, who is sent off with a red card. Now we have to play a man down the rest of the way, but Hope makes a spectacular diving stop of the PK by Cristiane, my old Red Stars teammate. This is an exhilarating turn of events — until the referee gives Brazil a rekick, apparently because Christie Rampone came in the box too soon. Marta converts the do-over to tie the game. Hope is ballistic. Nobody knows what is going on, because no explanation is forthcoming.

We press on and the game goes into overtime. Marta scores again with a looping left-footed volley over Hope's outstretched arm. Outmanned and almost out of time, we desperately push to keep our World Cup alive but are generating few threats. Abby gets the ball in the box but is denied as she turns to shoot. I have a good look from twenty yards out but launch it over the crossbar in the 121st minute. We might get one more chance, if we are lucky. Cristiane gets the ball in the left corner and holds the ball against Christie, dawdling, hoping for the whistle. Christie finally gets a piece of it, and Ali Krieger runs onto the loose ball and sends it to me in the middle. I take three touches up the middle of the field and slide it over to Rapinoe on the left flank. The whistle is going to blow any second.

Quick, Pinoe, let it fly, I think.

Pinoe does exactly that, launching a long cross to the far post. Abby is in the neighborhood, tracking it, timing it. She is closely marked. She goes up. Andreia, the Brazilian keeper, bounds off her line and goes up to punch it away. Defender Renata Costa, trying to get a body on Abby, goes up too. Abby gets to the ball first, though, snaps her head forward, and powers the ball into the near corner of the goal.

As the stadium erupts, Abby runs off to the corner and skids to her knees. It is the latest goal ever scored in the history of the Women's World Cup. It is about a million-to-one shot to tie the game the way we did, when we did.

Marta looks as if she has just gotten hit with a plank. Who can blame her? Pia huddles us up, and Paul Rogers chooses who will take the PKs and arranges the order. Paul works with us on PKs almost every day after practice and keeps track of our success rate. I am so ready. I can't imagine any way we can lose after Abby's miracle header.

Boxxy buries the first PK. I step up and do the same, and when Hope makes a stunning stop with an all-out dive to her left, we have the sliver of an opening we need. Ali Krieger finishes it off with a low shot just an inch or two inside the left post, and the party is on. Suddenly a team that was about to pack up and head home and get ripped for another World Cup disappointment has become America's soccer sweethearts.

Funny how that goes.

I am up until all hours and can barely sleep. When we meet the next day, the obvious first task is to put Brazil behind us and get ready for a semifinal against France in Monchengladbach, a city in western Germany, near the Dutch border and the River Rhine. Again we get off to an auspicious start, this time in the ninth minute, when I back-heel a ball up the sideline to Heather O'Reilly, who flashes down the flank and fires a cross that Lauren Cheney redirects for a dazzling finish. We don't sustain any momentum, though, as the French dice us up with their technical skill and quick passing game; they completely dominate the half, even if the scoreboard shows us with the lead.

The French square the game at one about ten minutes into the second half, which I start, almost inexplicably, with three giveaways in midfield. I haven't been off the field the whole tournament, but I come off now, Pia subbing me for Pinoe and moving Lauren Cheney into center midfield. I feel awful about this poor patch of play and am distraught that Pia wants me off the field. I feel as though I've let everybody down, and some of my old demons fire up like a blowtorch. I start feeling crappy about my whole World Cup. Pinoe is electric and makes things happen right away, leading to another header goal by Abby and an insurance goal by Alex Morgan to seal a 3–1 victory. That's the most important thing, but even as we celebrate, I am trying to fight off a funk.

"I really stunk it up tonight," I tell Brian afterwards.

Pia tells me to stay positive and think about simplifying things and keeping possession when we play the final against Japan, which beat home team Germany and then Sweden to make it to its first World Cup final.

"You have to let go of this and start preparing mentally for the final," James says. "I'm glad this happened now, and glad you got to rest a little because you are going to be fresh and you're going to play your best game of the tournament when it matters the most."

He too talks about keeping it simple, making good decisions, and not trying to produce a highlight-film play with each touch.

"Just be Carli," he says. James reminds me of his key points in the usual email he sends before big matches. This final isn't just big. It's massive, the most important game of my career.

At a final run-through before we play Japan, Hege Riise, Pia's assistant coach, approaches me during stretching.

"I am so excited for you in this game," she says. "You always come up big in finals. I know this is going to be your time to shine."

"Thanks, Hege. I want nothing more than to shine and bring this World Cup back to the States."

I am more nervous than I've ever been before a game on July 12, 2011, in Frankfurt, Germany. I have put France behind me, and I'm focusing completely on the next ninety minutes and heeding James's words.

Unlike so many other games this year, and in this tournament, we come out flying and make good on Pia's request to do better with possession. In the first minute Lauren Cheney gets behind the defense and just misses giving us an insanely quick lead. We are buzzing the Japanese goal like hornets, connecting passes, possessing the ball better than we ever have, the ball zipping cleanly from player to player, creating all kinds of chances against a side that normally does this sort of dictating. Abby has a great look but can't finish it. I get off a couple of dangerous shots but do not convert. Pinoe has a couple of prime chances, and Lauren has another one, but despite our domination, we cannot get on the board in the opening forty-five minutes.

I'm frustrated that we haven't broken through but feel so much better about my form and our collective level of play. Japan is about as skillful a team as there is in the world, and for half of a World Cup final its players are pretty much chasing us.

Keep on pushing. Keep on playing the same way, I tell myself. *It will come.*

And at last, in the sixty-ninth minute, it does. I am in a scrum near our 18-yard line, and I poke-check the ball free to Pinoe, who launches a beautiful fifty-yard ball to Alex Morgan, who makes a run straight toward the Japanese goal, her speed springing her free before she slots a leaning, left-footer into the far corner, her second goal in two games. It's a pretty good way to start a World Cup career for Alex, who is twenty-two and our youngest player.

The Japanese have had their best World Cup ever, and they've done it four months after an earthquake and tsunami devastated the country's northeast coast, killing almost 20,000 people and leaving thousands more homeless. One of Japan's professional teams had to cancel its season. All through the tournament, the Japanese coach and players said they hoped they might bring comfort and inspiration to their devastated homeland.

No, we do not think they are going to go away.

With under ten minutes to play, Japan takes advantage of a turnover in our end and a misplayed clearance and ties the score. The battle heads into two fifteen-minute extra time periods.

Pinoe and Alex team up again, and Alex launches a cross that Abby buries with a vintage header, putting us up 2–1, with under five minutes left. But then the Japanese answer again, this time with Homare Sawa, their captain who is playing in her fifth World Cup, who redirects a corner kick with a deft flick of her foot.

So it comes down to PKs again. Paul Rogers goes over the lineup, and Boxxy steps to the spot first. Ayumi Kaihori, the Japanese keeper, dives left and stops the ball with her foot. The Japanese shooter, Aya Miyama, who scored Japan's first goal, converts, and now it's my turn. I stride up to the 18, pick up the ball, and walk purposefully toward the spot, bouncing the ball twice as I go. I place it down and step back. I make my approach. I want to go to the upper left, the same direction as I went against Brazil, but with a little more power. I strike the ball well, but I am leaning back a bit and get under it.

I am sick almost the moment the ball leaves my foot. The ball skies over the crossbar. I can't believe it. I overhit it. I was so positive I would bury it. I rub my left hand over my face, turn away from the goal, and walk back to my teammates, never a fun walk to make. People say a few things to pick me up. They mean well, but it doesn't help much. Japan goes up 2–0, and now Tobin Heath is up. Tobin, who had come on for Pinoe, goes lower left, but Kaihori launches herself to the right and parries it away. We have taken three PKs and missed them all. Abby finally drills one in on her turn, and now it's on Japanese midfielder Saki Kumagai. If she makes it, Japan wins and we lose. If she misses, we have life.

Kumagai places the ball down and has to wait for Hope, who is trying to freeze her a bit, standing in her bright yellow uniform a few steps off the line. The referee tells her to get in the goal. Hope stretches her arms horizontally, as if she were a basketball player boxing somebody out, then raises her arms overhead and jumps up and down, trying to occupy every possible inch of space in the goal, trying to look as big and imposing as possible.

Saki Kumagai rips the ball into the upper left corner. Hope has no chance. The whole Japanese team runs out on the field. The emptiness I feel could fill oceans. If we have to lose, I'm glad it is to Japan, a country that has been through such a horrible ordeal, but that perspective mostly comes later. Now I can't get much beyond thinking I came up very small for my country. I know it is not just me. I know others missed, and that we win as a team and lose as a team. I just expect way more than this from myself.

"Don't worry," James says. "This is not going to define you. You are just going to keep getting better and better."

It is a hard night, a long night. Brian stays with me in the hotel, and it is great having him there. He says and does all the right things. I know how deeply he feels my pain because I see it on his face. I can't sleep. I keep replaying the PK. Maybe more than anything in my whole soccer career, I want that PK back. My golf pro boyfriend doesn't need to tell me: there are no mulligans in soccer.

12

Wonder in Wembley

EVEN IN DEFEAT, the U.S. Women's National Team is bigger than ever. Abby's epic goal against Brazil seems to have transfixed the whole country. The final game against Japan draws 13.5 million viewers, a soccer record for ESPN. Somebody tells me there were 7,000 tweets per second during the final. There were plenty of doubters after we lost to Sweden, but America loves a good comeback story, and we are that. Hundreds of fans are waiting at our Frankfurt hotel to welcome us, treating us as if we won the PK shootout. I do spots on *The Daily Show, Good Morning America,* and CNN. Abby, Hope, and Alex are the breakout stars, but all of us are much better known now than we were even a week earlier.

It's all good, but James has me convinced that I have much more improvement left in me, and that is entirely my focus. For years I have been doing a lot of fitness work on my own, beyond the national team workouts, because I know I need to. Now I am doing even more. At tournaments, I sneak out of hotels to get in a distance run. Or I knock out a set of 800-meter runs, supplementing them with push-ups and sit-ups and ab work. I want to be at my strongest when others are starting to falter. I want to be the American Steven Gerrard, setting up teammates, creating chances, orchestrating the attack with quick feet and inexhaustible energy.

The goal for 2012 is to peak at the London Olympics, and everything seems on course. We finish the Algarve Cup with a 4–0 thrashing of Sweden and then head to Japan for two friendlies, against Japan and Brazil. The day before the game against Japan, we tour the city of Sendai in the northeastern part of the country, one of the areas ravaged by the earthquake and tsunami almost exactly one year before. I look from the bus window at a vast expanse of wasteland, debris and shells of houses and battered boats planted on high ground, miles from the sea, where the earthquake started about fifteen miles beneath the floor. The nothingness goes on for miles. It is one of the most chilling spectacles I have ever seen. I can't even imagine what it must've been like to live through it. Soccer seems totally inconsequential when you think about the scope of this sort of destruction and the death of almost 20,000 people.

About six weeks before the Olympics, we play a friendly before a packed house at PPL Park in Chester, Pennsylvania. It's just across the Delaware River from my home, so I've got a bunch of family and friends there, though not my parents, of course. Four years since I was told to leave the house, I am still an ex-Lloyd in my parents' world. We're wearing our new red-striped "Where's Waldo" jerseys on a day so hot the pitch feels like a griddle. It's the Sunday of Memorial Day weekend.

Nothing memorable comes out of it for me.

Nothing memorable at all.

Not including a meaningless post–World Cup Victory Tour friendly in the fall of 2011, I have started forty-one straight games for the U.S. Women's National Team since returning from my broken ankle almost two years earlier. I get a rousing ovation when I am introduced to a hometown crowd before the game, and then I play forty-five forgettable minutes of football before Pia subs me out for Lauren Cheney.

Most of our team struggles through an uninspiring half; it's hard to believe we are the same side that played such strong, cohesive soccer in the World Cup final against Japan. We blast long balls up the field like rec players. Our back line gets panicky in the face of high Chinese pressure, and it spreads. We turn the ball over, make sloppy passes, leave openings for China to attack. Somehow we wind up with a 2–1 lead at the half, and I still can't tell you how.

Whether it's because I am trying too hard in front of my people, I don't know, but I am out of my element from the outset, losing the ball, playing helter-skelter, failing to convert two excellent chances inside the box. When Pia makes the switch, I am distraught. I am embarrassed. I go out with family and friends afterwards, but I have a hard time enjoying myself. I am in replay mode, maybe not as much as I was after I missed the PK against Japan, but close.

Jill Ellis, an assistant coach under Pia, knows me as well as any coach in the national program and knows my predilection for beating myself up. She texts me and tells me to keep my head up, reminding me it's one game and not to give it too much weight.

Dawn Scott, our fitness coach, also texts me.

"Keep fighting and move on," she says.

I head home for an eight-day break. I don't hear from James for three full days, which is very unusual. He tells me later that he wanted me to sweat it out for a bit and think about my mistakes. I spend the time training hard and thinking harder. I am doing an upper-body workout in my garage when I finally hear from him. I'm still beating myself up, and it's in that moment that I realize that I can't have anyone at my events anymore. It changes things. I put too much pressure on myself to please people. I know I shouldn't, but I do. Brian is planning on coming to London for the Olympics.

"Please don't," I tell him. "I hope you understand it's not about you. It's about me."

My mind continues to race:

I can't believe that it's still possible for me to have a game like this, after all the work I've put in. I thought I was beyond this point. I hate it. I hate that it's staying with me. Hate that it's affecting my confidence.

We leave for a trip to Sweden and two games against the Swedes and the Japanese. In our first training session, I don't feel well. I do okay, but mentally I might as well be in Greenland. I don't even want the ball. I haven't felt like this in a long time.

Jill keeps trying to lift me up. One day Pia calls me up to her room to talk.

"What do you think went on in the China game?" she asks.

"I don't know, I was just off that day, and it was weird because I had been doing really well in training. I'm human. It was just one of those days, I guess."

"Well, I just want you to know I believe in you one hundred percent," Pia says. "If there is anything I can do to help you when your game is a bit off, please let me know."

"I will. Thanks," I say.

We have a couple days off from training, and I run both days. Before the first game, Pia wants to talk again. She comes in my room and tells me that I am not starting.

"Cheney has been doing well, and she deserves to start," Pia says. "But it's going to be you and Boxxy and Cheney in the midfield during the Olympics, and we're going to need all three of you. Just stay ready and make the most of your chance when it comes."

Though I can't say I am shocked by this news, it is still tough to hear. I know I had a poor first half against China. I still think Pia is overreacting. I've been a fixture on this team for a couple of years. I've come up big in important moments. To get yanked from the lineup because of one bad half seems extreme.

I do not tell Pia that. I sit on the bench, smoldering. When Pia calls for me to replace Boxxy, I do everything I'm supposed to do. I sit back and defend and tackle hard, play some good balls, and create chances. We win 3–1, and then we play Japan and I don't start again. Pia comes up to me in the locker room beforehand and is smiling and laughing and puts her arm on my shoulder.

"How are you?" she says.

"I'm great," I say.

"Watch Cheney and Boxxy. You are going to come in at halftime."

I am still angry and play with an edge when I come on in the second half. I work hard on both sides of the ball. We win 4–1, and I can't wait to get on the plane and get back home so I can work with James and train my butt off and prove to Pia she should never have taken me out of the starting lineup. Sometimes I have to work hard to find a slight to motivate me. I don't have to work hard at all this time.

I am going to show Pia Sundhage.

We head out to Sandy, Utah, for our last friendly before we head to London for the Olympics. Pia must be enjoying these meetings with me because she calls for another one.

"What do you think of your last two games?" she says.

"I think I did what I needed to do when I came on," I say.

"What do you think you need to do to get back in the starting lineup?" she asks.

"The same things I have been doing," I say.

"How would you compare yourself to Lauren Cheney as a player?" she says.

This strikes me as a very odd question, an inappropriate question. I don't know what she wants to hear from me. I just tell her the truth.

"First of all, Cheney and I are completely different players with different strengths. Second of all, I don't like to worry about other people or compare myself to them. I worry about myself and what I can bring to the team."

Pia nods approvingly and again seems as if she wants to build me up.

"You were the best player we had in qualifying. I hope you know that," she says.

I thank her, and before I leave I want to tell her one more thing — that the bad half against China was not going to define me, any more than the missed PK was going to define me.

"It hurt my confidence, and I held on to it for a long time — too long — but I am fine now, and I am ready to fight back," I tell her. "I won't let you or the team down. I will fight and keep fighting, and I will win this battle."

Pia's jaw drops, in an almost cartoonish way. I don't know why.

Maybe she's impressed that I said all the right things. Who knows? She tells me again that she is going to need all three of us in midfield, and that sometimes I may play with Boxxy, other times with Lauren. Sometimes I will be attacking, and other times I may have to sit back and mostly defend.

"I'm ready to do whatever needs to be done," I say.

I return home from Utah for one last blast of training with James and go at it as hard as ever. I land on Saturday and am on the field playing against a Universal Soccer Academy boys' team a day later. All week I do what James calls "physical power" training, with sets of sprints from 100 meters up to 800 meters, along with hill work, upper-body circuits, and distance runs every day. Heather Mitts, my teammate and fellow Universal Soccer student, is doing some fine-tuning with James and thinks I am overdoing it in a big way.

"You aren't going to be able to get through the Olympics if you keep up this pace," Heather tells me. "You will never last. You are going to burn out. I really think you need to back off."

I know Heather means well, and I know I must look like a maniac, pushing so hard before the biggest tournament of the year. But I also know this is exactly what I need . . . for my mind as well as my body.

I don't let up once I get to England. I have to secretly go out and do these workouts. My first full day there is an off day for the team. I go for a ten-mile run and then the next day do three three-minute runs at 70 percent effort, 80 percent, and then 90 percent — nine runs in total, all on a treadmill. I also do doggie sprints behind a building near our hotel after a training session in the evening. We have a team outing to a medieval castle. It's cool, but I am too tunneled in on the present to wrap my head around the Middle Ages. When we get back, Pia comes into my room and officially lets me know what I already know . . . that I will not be starting in our first game, against France.

"This is not about you doing anything wrong. You've been playing well. We're going to need you, so stay ready," she says.

"I'm ready," I say.

James tells me, "If you want to be ready — truly ready — then you need to start visualizing. Start the process a few days before the game. Be quiet and centered with mental images of playing this game against France. See yourself on the field. See the game unfolding in your mind. Trust me, it will make a big difference."

So I start visualizing more intently than I ever have in my life. I sit in my room, shut my eyes, listen to the music, and visualize. I go on walks and visualize. I visualize that our team is down against France and I come on to score the winning goal.

All the extra work, mental and physical, has done just what I hoped it would. I feel strong and fit and confident again. We have a scrimmage against Norway and we win 2–0, and I am on top of my game, getting lots done.

"You were awesome today, Carli," Heather tells me.

"Thanks. I feel good," I say.

We travel up to Glasgow, Scotland, for our opener against France, and it starts about as badly as it can. We fall behind 2–0 in the opening fourteen minutes, and then Boxxy goes down a couple of minutes later. She's been battling a calf injury for the past few weeks now, and you could see in training that she was not 100 percent. Boxxy tries to gut it out, but the grimace on her face makes it obvious there is no way she can continue.

Pia summons me off the bench, and after the briefest of warm-ups, I am in our Olympic midfield sooner than I ever imagined. Abby scores on a header off of a Pinoe corner, and Alex pops a bouncing ball over the French keeper's head, and we're even before the half is over.

Playing holding mid, I am careful not to do too much or get caught upfield too far. I am keeping my touches to a minimum, focusing on strong tackling and clean passes. Ten minutes into the second half, Pinoe tracks down a loose ball that the French have given away, near the right sideline. I am pushing upfield, with some space in front of me, and when Pinoe sees it she delivers a perfect square ball to my feet. I settle in with my right foot and follow with a quick one-two that ends with a flick with the outside of my right foot, and in an instant I am clear of a closing defender. I have just enough room, about twenty-five yards out on the right, and I let it rip. Baseball sluggers talk about how great it feels when they hit a ball in their sweet spot. This ball is in my sweet spot. It rises like a tracer and rockets into the upper left corner of the net. We're up 3–2. I run toward the U.S. bench and go into a skid and get hugs from Pinoe and everybody.

"I wanted to show the bench some love," I joked to a reporter later.

Alex scores another goal off a scramble in front, and we've answered another challenge in a big way. Afterwards, somebody asks Pia about the impact I had and she says, "She changed the game. She didn't start the game, but she finished the game."

Back in my room, I have my own perspective.

I guess this visualization stuff works, I think.

After a typically exciting tournament night — ice bath, stretch, hydrate — I go for a light twenty-minute run the next day to loosen up and get ready for our second game, against Colombia, a rapidly improving team with several extremely dangerous players. Colombia comes at us with feet flying — and with sucker punches too. (Abby Wambach does not get her black eye on the handshake line.) It's a chippy game, but you can't get lured into payback or playing with reckless anger. The best revenge is always to win. In the thirty-third minute, Pinoe strikes a high, bending ball from distance after Alex picks a Colombian pocket, and Abby makes it 2–0 with a sliding, angled right-footer with under twenty to play. I have spent the whole game doing my midfield housekeeping, winning balls and distributing the ball quickly. Just a few minutes after Abby's goal, I play a ball ahead to Lauren Cheney, who finds Pinoe to her right. I see a channel up the middle in front of me, and off I go, a full sprint into space. Pinoe tucks a perfect ball on the floor to me, in stride, and after a touch in the box, I slide it under the onrushing keeper into the left side of the goal.

Two games ago, I was a veteran who had lost her starting spot and whose Olympic role was murkier than the English Channel. Now we have two victories behind us and I have two goals behind me.

Chester, Pennsylvania?

I don't even remember playing a game there.

After winning a hard-fought battle with North Korea on a goal by Abby, we move into the quarterfinals against New Zealand. It's another scrappy game, and I am a bit off at the outset, but I play my way into the game and keep up my high work rate from box to box. Abby finishes a pass from Alex to give us a 1–0 lead in the twenty-seventh minute and then, with about twenty minutes left to play, I settle a bouncing ball and take a touch as I start upfield. I see an opening up the middle, where Alex is making a run. I chip a forty-yard ball, and Alex gets in behind the defense and is alone on the Kiwi keeper, Jenny Bindon, who rushes off her line and goes into a slide, with Alex sprinting at her full blast. Alex tries to leap over her, but her left knee slams into Bindon's face, and the two of them go sprawling as the ball trickles away. The keeper takes the worst of it, by far, but Alex has to come off. Pia replaces her with Sydney Leroux. Alex is one of those strikers who scores in bunches; when she is confident and making those galloping runs of hers, she can be a huge threat, and with seven goals in our last eight games, she is in a good place right now. We don't want to lose her, for sure, but Syd steps right in and buries her first Olympic goal to seal a 2–0 victory.

It's not our prettiest game, but we keep advancing, and Hope and the defense deliver our third straight shutout. We move into the semifinals with Canada in Old Trafford, home of Manchester United and one of the most storied soccer stadiums in the world. The Canadians know us well, and they are playing at a high level under their new coach, John Herdman. Nobody forgets the scrap they gave us in our overtime victory in the quarterfinals in the Beijing Games, and they have the ever-dangerous Christine Sinclair.

Three different times in Old Trafford, Sinclair gives Canada a one-goal lead. Three times, we answer. The game seems to get more intense by the minute. It is not always a showcase for the Olympic ideals. In the fifty-fifth minute, I am on the ground in the box, and suddenly there is a foot stomping on my head, driving my head into the pitch.

It's as dirty a play as you will ever see. A stud on the bottom of the boot slams into my temple, maybe an inch from my eye. The culprit is Canadian veteran Melissa Tancredi, who commits seven fouls in the game, including one in the first minute. Tancredi's foot stomp — which should've been a red card — somehow goes unnoticed.

I get up and keep going, and that's what our team does too. Pinoe scores our first two goals, the first one on a curling corner kick that sneaks inside the near post and the second on a wicked, angled strike from distance. We're still down a goal in the seventy-eighth minute when Erin McLeod, the Canadian goalkeeper, goes up to grab a corner kick and falls to the ground to secure it. McLeod, like virtually all keepers, often takes longer than the six seconds the rules allow a keeper to get rid of the ball. Abby is counting loudly — "One, two, three, four . . ." to make sure that the referee, Christina Pedersen of Norway, is aware of McLeod's tardiness. McLeod dribbles the ball a few times and lets go with a dropkick, and Pedersen blows her whistle.

Nobody knows what is going on, until it becomes apparent Pedersen has called McLeod for delay of game, giving us an indirect kick. I have never seen this call made in a game, let alone a game of this magnitude. I am not worrying about it, though. I got my head stomped and there was no call.

The ref owes us one.

Tobin Heath touches the ball on the kick, and Pinoe rips a blast toward goal. As Canadian defender Marie-Eve Nault turns away to shield her face from the shot, it caroms off her arm. Pedersen blows her whistle again, this time for a PK. The Canadians are enraged. Abby is calm, stepping to the spot and knocking a low shot inside the left post to tie the game, her fifth goal in five Olympic games.

Abby very nearly wins it for us about six minutes later, when Alex makes a cross from the left flank, toward the right of the goal. Abby is crashing the net hard and gets the ball on her foot, and I am sure the ball is going in the net, but Abby's sliding shot veers just wide of the near post and into overtime the semifinal goes.

All I can think of as we prepare for two fifteen-minute overtimes is that this is what I train for, to be able to keep pushing on, finding gears I don't know I have. In games like this, where the outcome can swing on the smallest of events — a tackle at midfield, a high-pressure run that forces a sloppy pass, a sprint to keep a ball in bounds — the last thing I ever want is to feel I didn't leave it all out there. It's a cliché, I know: give it your all, never say die . . . all of that.

But you know what?

This is exactly what winning championships takes . . . keeping the foot on the pedal even when you are on your last drop of gas. So I dig deep. We all dig deep. I can't tell you for sure that we want this game more than the Canadians, because their players have shown great heart the whole game, but I can tell you this:

We are going to do whatever it takes to win. We won't stomp on any Canadian heads, but we will battle to the end.

Near the end of the first overtime, Canada's Diana Matheson makes a good run down the right side and crosses to Sinclair, who is gunning for number four when Rachel Buehler breaks it up just in time, forcing a corner kick. At the end of the next overtime, and after good chances for both teams, Alex gets space and arches a cross to Abby. Abby goes up. I feel as though I've seen this movie a thousand times in my career. I know the ending by heart:

Abby goes higher than anybody else, using all of her height and power and skill.

Abby's forehead meets the airborne ball.

Abby snaps her head forward.

The ball rips into the goal.

All of that happens, except the last part: Abby's header bounds off the crossbar. The game stays tied. We move into the third minute of extra time, 123 minutes into the match, when Heather O'Reilly, who came on for Lauren Cheney in the 101st minute, gets off a cross from the right side. There is a crowd in front. I see Alex measure it and go up, a pink headband rising above the fray, connecting with the ball, knocking a looping header right over McLeod's hand, into the net.

It is our first lead of the whole game, and a very good time to get it

— seconds before Pedersen looks at her watch and signals the game's end.

The Canadians are understandably bitter, especially Sinclair, who was so brilliant throughout.

"We feel like we didn't lose, we feel like it was taken from us," Sinclair tells the media later. "It's a shame in a game like that that was so important, the ref decided the result before it started."

I'm not buying the conspiracy theory, and not giving it a moment's thought. We have more important things ahead of us — such as a return engagement with Japan. In the 2007 World Cup, we lost to the Brazilians and then got another shot at them in Beijing in the Olympic gold medal game.

In 2011 we lost to the Japanese in the World Cup, and now we get another shot at them in the final in London. It's the same scenario that we had with Brazil in 2007 and 2008. I like the symmetry.

Wembley Stadium is one of those holy places in sports, a building you walk into and feel the history pouring out of every one of the 90,000 red seats. The current Wembley only dates to 2007, but it's on the same patch of North London land as its predecessor, still home to the English national team and still the site of the biggest football game of the year in England, the Football Association (FA) Challenge Cup championship. So, to me, Wembley is Wembley.

And I am thrilled and honored to be here.

After a day of rest following the Canada marathon, we have a light training session and go over final preparations for the Japanese. It's our fourth meeting of the year against them, so there don't figure to be any major surprises. We know how good the Japanese are on the ball and how they like to attack defenses in precise, quick-footed waves. They are masters of the one-touch pass, and we have to stay organized.

The biggest adjustment for me in this final is returning to my regular position as an attacking midfielder. Boxxy's injury has healed, and she has returned to the lineup at holding mid, so that frees me up to attack more. I am all for that.

Maybe it's the historic setting, or the gold medal on the line, or the expectations I have now that I am back at attacking mid, but I am a bundle of nerves for this Olympic final. I have hardly been nervous at all in the previous games. Now it's as if every nerve ending in my body is plugged in.

We board the team bus from the Olympic Village, and I head to my usual seat, a couple of rows from the back on the right. Hope is in the seat across from me, the way she always is. When you look at team photos, especially candid ones, Hope and I always seem to be next to each other, and it's no accident; the bond we forged through the World Cup ordeal five years before only gets stronger. More than anybody else on the team, she is there for me, and I know she always will be. That counts for everything in my world.

We arrive at Wembley about ninety minutes before kickoff. James, of course, has sent me his usual get-your-mind-right email. It centers me and calms me. I reread it on the bus. It's almost a meditative exercise by now, like listening to a harp or the sound of the sea. It's so easy before big games for your mind to race and get so cluttered that you go out and try to do way too much.

Here's what James says:

Ms. Lloyd,

I felt that I owe you another email. The purpose of my previous email was to keep you focused and set your mind to work on a day-by-day type of thinking program. As it turns out that strategy worked to perfection and you were able to not only meet all the goals I set for you but you actually crushed all the goals I set for you.

*Today is another day and new goals are set for you. Your goal for today is to blank out the world and zone in on everything that is happening between the lines on the field. To blank out everything and be **the hardest worker, the quickest thinker, the most efficient, most creative and most dangerous player on the field.***

I know that these goals may seem like a lot but they are really not. They are not because it's what you have been doing, with the exception of "most dangerous." Because of your defensive role you have had the opportunity to be "the hardest worker, the quickest thinker, the most efficient and most creative" and now with the at-tacking role you have been presented the opportunity to add the "most dangerous" tag onto your already super impressive showing at this Olympics.

I know adding the "most dangerous" tag onto the list is not hard as I know that this is not the Lloyd of the 2011 World Cup. This Lloyd is fitter, stronger, smarter, leaner and way more efficient than 2011. In 2011 they faced a Lloyd that was in a tug of war battle be-tween the Women's Professional Soccer League and WNT and with me for limited time and I was not able to run the true program I wanted to run. This year I had you all to myself and I know what I built. I have actually built the best player in the World. No other player in the world has done what you have done and none of them are better than you on 8/9/2012. On this day you are the best in the world and you need to get out there and show the world who you are. You are in form and top of your game. Peaking!!!!!

Show them what you have been doing for the last ten years and show them that you are the most complete player on the planet. That you can do it all! Defend like no other and attack like no other. You go ahead and show them. Your body will not let you down and your mind will never give up and push you more than every player on that field.

Today is the day you close the second phase saying, "I gave you a glimpse in Phase 1. You didn't believe in me but I proved you wrong in Phase 2. But you won't be able to get enough of me in Phase 3."

*Remember this? "This is your time to shine and you will **keep shining day by day** until you once again shine the brightest." The brightest is today. So bright the doubters will never forget it! So bright your opponents will tremble! So bright your legacy will never be forgotten!*

Let's go get this, Ms. Lloyd. Let's go own this game. Make it ours.
                                                    James Galanis

I walk off the bus, headphones in place, listening to Chris Brown's "Dreamer" as I go. It lifts me up. We file into the locker room. It's spa-cious and bright and has a pink LONDON 2012 logo on the floor. It is big-time. I have a corner locker, next to Heather O'Reilly, my long-time Jersey pal and teammate. After I get dressed, I walk out of the locker room and down a corridor, into a tunnel, which leads me to as famous a soccer pitch as there is in the world. I am breathless. It is immense and perfect and even more beautiful than I imagined it would be.

I cannot wait to play on it.

Back in the locker room, minutes before we are to walk out, the coaches leave the room. Pia has gone over strategic stuff in a meeting the night before, reminding us to apply high pressure, tackle hard, win fifty-fifty balls, be strong in the air, and use our size to our advantage. We know against such a technically superb team as Japan its players will almost certainly control possession in the game.

"Don't worry about that," Pia says. "Let's just stay organized defensively, and we will be fine."

Pia isn't one to give rah-rah speeches, or any other sort of speech. She leaves us on our own, and we all huddle up. Christie Rampone, our captain, talks, and then Abby talks and a few others chime in. I don't say anything. All I want to do is get on the pitch and play.

We file out of the locker room, high-five the staff as we head down the hallway, and get lined up for the pregame walkout. I am hand in hand with a little blond girl, and when we step onto the pitch I cannot believe the size of the crowd. More than 80,000 people, the largest crowd ever to see a women's soccer game, are in those red seats. It is a staggering sight, a beautiful sight. They are here to see us, to see women play soccer. I am a jumble of energy and anticipation. We shake hands and listen to the two national anthems, and now, finally, it is time.

When the whistle blows, I feel almost as if I am a bull who has just been let loose on the streets of Pamplona.

I am so ready.

We kick off, and Abby rolls the ball to Alex, who plays it back to me. Pia likes us to play long ball at the start, maybe to help us get our legs pumping and blood going, so I send it long upfield toward

Abby. Barely a minute in, I intercept a pass for Japan's great mid-fielder, Homare Sawa, and off we go on the counterattack. I don't make much of a cross at the end of it, but starting the game with a strong defensive play always stokes me up even more.

In the eighth minute, Japan makes an uncharacteristic mistake and loses an easy ball out of bounds. Pinoe throws in to Boxxy, who slides the ball crossfield to Kelley O'Hara, who pushes it on to Tobin, who makes a run down the left flank and makes a nice pass inside the box to Alex, who gets instant separation, sprints to the end line, and makes a great cross. I see this unfolding near the 18 and make a hard run toward the goal, leaving my mark behind. Abby is in front, ready to finish. I see Alex's ball floating toward me and keep running hard toward the goal. The cross is sinking fast. Abby, to my right, has her left leg raised, ready to side volley it in, though a defender is right on her. I have a clear lane in front of me and see the ball coming at me, as big as a beach ball. I lower my head, hit the ball squarely, and drive it into the net.

Most people think Abby scored until they see the replay. Abby and I actually joked that I stole her goal. I go running and sliding in cel-ebration, arms outstretched, and soon my teammates are on top of me. It is a dream beginning. We are on the board and ready for more.

The Japanese have started tentatively, but they are firing up fast. In the seventeenth minute, Christie Rampone saves a goal after a defensive breakdown with a brilliant block with her right foot, and Hope follows by stuffing the rebound. It's a close call, and Hope is even better just over a minute later, when Japan's Yuki Ogimi puts a head on a cross and launches it toward our goal. The game is an instant away from being tied, but Hope dives and punches the ball into the crossbar. Ojimi tries to pound in rebound but misses wide. Hope has saved us again. Japan keeps the pressure on, its attack now humming. Aya Miyama, the Japanese captain, pounds a ball into the crossbar in the thirty-fourth minute, and we dodge another bullet.

None of us ever thought this would be easy.

Ten minutes into the second half, Pinoe plays a square ball to me not far from midfield. I take a touch and see a stretch of space in front of me, with only one defender to beat. So I take off with the ball, veering to the right. I take two more touches, and then a few more, and I still have room. Still going right, I notice the defense, and the goal-keeper, are all going with me, and at that moment I know it is time.

I am about twenty-five yards out. I take a final touch and let it rip, across my body, across the grain. I hit it squarely. I watch the ball's flight, watch it all the way until it flies into the side netting, just inside the left post.

Wembley explodes in noise. I run around looking for people to hug.

We are up 2–0.

There are thirty-five minutes to play, an eternity and a half. Nobody believes this is done. Nobody. The Japanese came back twice in the World Cup, and there is no way they are quitting now. The Japanese are pushing the attack, committing numbers in the offensive third. Ojimi converts a rebound with a side-footed shot that Hope has no chance on in the sixty-fourth minute, and it is 2–1. Japan keeps coming. We try to stay tight and organized. In the eighty-second minute, Lauren Cheney pushes a left-footed pass to me, and I have space and let it fly, a left-footed laser that feels good when it leaves my foot but sails inches over the crossbar.

Damn.

That could've clinched it.

It's a one-goal game, and the most skillful team in the world is coming at us. In the eighty-third minute, Mana Iwabuchi, a nine-teen-year-old forward, pressures Christie Rampone as she is receiving a pass, steals it, and goes in alone on Hope. Iwabuchi takes a left-footed touch, then a right, and then side-foots a shot toward the far post, from maybe ten yards away. It looks to be a certain goal, a tie game. Hope sees Iwabuchi, sees the ball on the side of her right foot, reads it perfectly. Iwabuchi kicks toward the far post. Hope dives to her left. She knocks it toward the corner.

It is a world-class save. Hope has had several of them in this game. She is the best in the world, and this is why.

Hope has to smother a dangerous cross in the next minute, and you just know it's going to be frantic right until the final whistle. The game goes into extra time, and now it's the ninety-second minute and Japan is making its last push. A forward named Karina Maruyama gets the ball on the right and starts to attack, and I make a hard run at her, contesting her advance, getting in her way enough so that she trips me. The referee blows the whistle for a foul. Hope takes the ensuing free kick and sends it far downfield. The ball never returns to our end. The three whistles sound. The crowd roars.

We are Olympic champions, again.

We hug and cry and revel, and I look up at this massive, holy place we are in — Wembley — and disbelief only begins to describe it. We have just defended our Olympic gold medal.

In Wembley Stadium.

Could it get better than this?

The medal ceremony is one of the greatest moments of my life. I listen to "The Star-Spangled Banner" and even though we won in 2008, somehow this is so much richer, so much better. I love our team and love how we fought, and on a personal note, I feel so much satisfaction, knowing that I started the Olympic Games as a reserve and finished them in a whole different place.

This isn't about me, though. It's about a group of women who fought hard and gave every morsel of energy and skill they had to offer. It's about sacrifice and belief and never giving in, never giving up. It's about character — one of the Five Pillars James has talked to me about from the start. When a reporter asks James about my performance in London, he says, "Carli has achieved so much, and she trains as if she's achieved almost nothing. That is a very rare quality."

Later, somebody asks Pia about her decision to bench me to start the Olympics.

"She proved that I was wrong," Pia replies. "I am really happy that she is more clever than I am."

Long-range strikes are one of my favorite parts of the game. Here I tee one up against Japan in London.

One of my all-time-favorite celebration photos. It's a happy pile of players when we took the lead against Japan in the Olympic final in London.

Arm in arm with my best friend on the team, Hope Solo, minutes after we beat Japan for the Olympic gold in 2012.

When we won gold in London, it was show-and-tell time with our new medals.

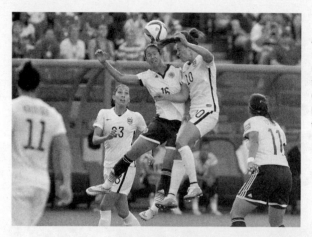

A full-service midfielder has to do it all. Here I go up for a header against Colombia in the knockout round of the 2015 World Cup.

Not too many people thought we'd beat Germany in the World Cup semifinals. My PK got us on the board—and on our way to a 2–0 victory.

You think I was pumped at all after my first goal in the 2015 World Cup final? Check out the bulging veins.

The Cup final was three minutes old when my first goal came to rest.

The celebration was on after I scored number 2 against Japan in Vancouver.

When the great Abby Wambach came on late in the World Cup final, it was only right that I take off the captain's armband and present it to her.

Jill Ellis gets a major bear hug after the World Cup final.

There's nothing better than being on top of the podium and bringing the World Cup trophy back home after sixteen years.

The stuff of dreams: holding up the Golden Ball after being named the best player in the 2015 World Cup.

I was happy to win the Silver Boot as the second leading scorer in the 2015 World Cup, but nothing came close to winning the Cup itself.

A happy reunion of family and friends greeted me at the Newark airport on my return from the London Olympics in 2012. That's my former teammate Heather Mitts to my immediate right.

The ultimate World Cup celebration: a ticker-tape parade in New York City with Megan Rapinoe and, of course, the trophy!

My future husband, Brian Hollins, and I have prime seats at the 2015 ESPYs in Los Angeles.

President Barack Obama graciously invited the World Cup champions to the White House. He seems quite pleased with his new jersey.

USWNT coach Jill Ellis and I were honored by FIFA as World Coach and World Player of the Year at a Swiss gala in January 2016. Playing for Jill has been one of the best things that has ever happened to me.

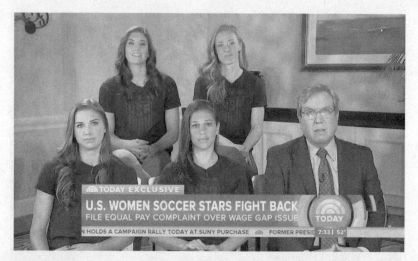

In the spring of 2016, my U.S. teammates (from left) Alex Morgan, Hope Solo, and Becky Sauerbrunn, and I (along with Megan Rapinoe, not pictured) filed a federal wage-discrimination complaint. That's our attorney, Jeffrey Kessler, on the right.

I love working with young players. Here I do a live demo of the drills I still do to this day at my camp.

13

Coaching Carousel

I ARRIVE HOME FROM THE OLYMPICS still in a full state of euphoria, with my second gold medal around my neck and my first and only boyfriend, Brian Hollins, waiting for me at Newark Liberty Airport. My aunt Patti and uncle Wayne, cousins Jaime and Adam, and Jaime's husband and their two kids are all there. So are my aunt Sandy and Brian's mother and sister and her husband and their two kids, along with my best friends, twin sisters Kathy and Karen Sweet, and friend Laura Aleszczyk. (James isn't there, but that's only because he prefers to sit out the revelry and let me celebrate with my family and friends.) They've arranged for a party bus to take us all back down the Turnpike to my place in Mount Laurel, which they've decorated with an American flag, posters, and USA placards. There are red-white-and-blue hearts and a homemade sign that reads: WE ARE SO PROUD OF YOU CARLI. Everyone is wearing either a number 10 jersey or an Olympic shirt or a T-shirt with a silhouette of me kicking a ball.

It's a small and heartfelt celebration, just the way I like it.

My parents and brother and sister are not part of the festivities, by their own choice. I don't hear from any of them after the Olympics, though they do send me a card. It's hard to believe that it has been four years since we've had any relationship to speak of. Things are no closer to being resolved than they were in 2008, and in some ways they are even worse, as articles start to appear talking about how James's training methods helped forge an Olympic champion. Everything seemed to change once James began to be credited for playing a huge role in my development.

As I said before, I never would've gotten close to the national team, or James Galanis, without my parents' support. There is plenty of credit to go around. It's all so crazy and needless, and so sad, but after all this time I am getting resigned to it. I would be thrilled if all this went away tomorrow and we could be whole again. I will meet my parents wherever I have to meet them. I will own my part in it. James has encouraged me over and over again to find a solution, to reach a détente.

He does it when I get back from London, in fact.

"You need to reach out to your parents. You both made mistakes, and you need to find a way to try to reunite with your family," he says. "Reach out to them and be open. You can fix this. Sit down and have an honest conversation and put it behind you."

A few weeks after I return from London, my brother reaches out and wants to come over. It's awkward at first. We make small talk. Then we get to bigger issues.

"I just want you to know how much this hurts Mom and Dad every single day of their lives," Stephen says. "They want you back in the worst way. I just hope you can see how unfair you've been with them."

He goes on to say, "You don't give yourself enough credit. You were destined to be this sort of player, an Olympic champion."

This is Lloyd family code for: "You give James too much credit for your success."

Stephen stays for a couple of hours. I don't see much change going on, but he asks if I would consider getting together with Mom and Dad.

"I'm going to think about it," I say.

I decide to invite my parents over to my house. I've been in it for over four years, and they've never really even seen it.

My parents come over a couple of weeks after I visit with my brother. We start with chitchat, but we all know we're not here to talk about how lovely an autumn it has been.

"I am sorry that I've been disrespectful at times," I say. "I was wrong to be that way after all that you've done for me."

"I am sorry I snapped that day when I told you to move out," my father says. We are off to a pretty good start. I allow myself to be hopeful. If we can at least respect each other's feelings instead of trying to shoot them down, we can get somewhere. If both sides can own their hurtful behavior, we have a chance.

I give my parents a tour of my home, upstairs and downstairs. "It's so nice," my mom says. "We're so proud of what you're doing and that you can live in such a beautiful home." They sit on my couch, and we start to talk, and I own up to just about everything they have had an issue with. I find out, finally, about my dad's heart surgery and how he had a 90 percent blockage and had to be rushed to the hospital. He tells me he's been under lots of stress at work and with our family situation, but he was lucky to get it taken care of right away. All in all, it's as good a visit as we've had in a long time. My dad has to get up early for work, so they leave after a few hours.

"We'll reach out and get together again soon," my mother says.

"That sounds good," I say, and then I hug each of them and say good-bye.

When they leave, I have a feeling I haven't had for a long time in regard to my family. I have hope.

Things may be taking a turn toward the stable with the family, but not so on the team. Pia Sundhage is out as coach. It is announced on September 1, 2012, in Rochester, New York, Abby's hometown, hours before we are set to begin our victory tour against Costa Rica. It is twenty-three days after Pia led us to our second Olympic gold medal. Pia, true to form, used the moment to break into song before the crowd, this time Dylan's "If Not for You."

With a five-year record of 89-6-10, Pia is returning home to coach the national team of her native Sweden and says she is "so happy." She praises all of us and thanks us and her assistants for making her look good.

"Before I took this job, I always admired the spirit and character of the U.S. team, but to experience that firsthand on the training field and from the bench as their coach was truly special and something I will treasure for the rest of my life," Pia said.

U.S. Soccer president Sunil Gulati is no less gushing about Pia and says it was an awfully difficult decision whether to let her go. Everybody wants to make it sound as if Pia was the one who engineered the change, but I'm not so sure, since that's usually not how things work around the U.S. Women's National Team. April Heinrichs was forced out by a core of veterans who basically ran the team, and Greg Ryan was too, though he was going to be a goner anyway the moment the terrible 2007 World Cup ended.

Pia met with Sunil after London, and from what I understand, they talked about her future before tabling the discussion and deciding to meet again in a few weeks. In the interim, a so-called leadership group of players had a conference call and began to quietly push Sunil to get rid of Pia. When word leaks out on the team about what is going on, I am upset, and so are lots of other people who aren't part of the "leadership group." I don't know how everything goes down. I just know that Sunil and Dan Flynn, CEO of U.S. Soccer, fly in and meet with us before the Costa Rica game and talk to us about the situation, and soon the announcement is made that Pia is leaving and is "so happy" about her dream opportunity back in Sweden.

Pia and I have had our differences here and there — I was furious when I was benched before the Olympics — but I still have great respect for her as a coach. She is positive and clever and humble, and she made us a much better and more creative team. People forget that she took over a team in complete chaos after the 2007 World Cup, that she gradually brought Hope back into the fold and stabilized things. Two Olympic golds and a runner-up finish on PKs in the World Cup final is a pretty good body of work in five years.

I am going to miss Pia Sundhage.

• • •

The best year I've ever had in soccer ends in the saddest of ways when I learn that my old Medford Strikers coach, Joe Dadura, has passed away suddenly at the age of fifty-six. I am about to leave for our final games of 2012, a three-game series against China in Detroit, Houston, and Boca Raton, but push back my flight so I can attend Mr. D's funeral. The last decade of Mr. D's life was not easy, in any way, ever since he was hit in the predawn hours by a drunk driver not far from a Taco Bell in West New York, New Jersey. Mr. D was making a work delivery. The driver supposedly had been out drinking and fell asleep at the wheel. Mr. D was standing beside his truck and had no chance. He suffered horrible injuries and battled them to the end, which came nine years later.

The funeral is in a tall brick building with white pillars in Washington Township, New Jersey. Most of our old Medford Strikers team is there. It is not a reunion we wanted to have. There are touching tributes and photo montages of Mr. D, many of the images showing him in his red-and-black Strikers jacket. He was almost never without it. We hug Kacy, our teammate and Mr. D's daughter, and Mrs. D, and we share memories of all the practices and tournaments we had with Mr. D, who started the team and made it into a powerhouse. It is still the closest team I've ever been on, and still the purest fun I have ever had playing soccer. Mr. D made it that way. We felt so much joy playing together. We loved each other, and we loved our coach.

I sign the memorial book and write, "I will forever cherish all the wonderful moments we had together. Thank you, Mr. D, for everything you did for me."

After saying good-bye to my former teammates, I get on a plane to Detroit. A few days later, we are playing China at Ford Field, and in the fiftieth minute I knife through a crowd in the box and pound a low, left-footed drive inside the near post. It breaks a scoreless tie, and I run upfield thinking of one thing:

That was for you, Mr. D.

Our new coach — number three during my time with the team — takes over on January 1, 2013. He is a fifty-eight-year-old Scotsman named Tom Sermanni. He coached Australia to three World Cup quarterfinal finishes and helped make the Australians a much more skillful and technically proficient team. Tom also coached in our defunct pro league, the WUSA, and is known for a laid-back temperament and for being a players' coach, a man who lets players play and treats people like grown-ups.

Tom has strong credentials and seems to be a very nice man, and if you are going to make a coaching change, this is the time to do it — with no truly major tournaments coming up until the 2015 World Cup in Canada.

We begin our 2013 with a training camp in Jacksonville, Florida, in early February. Tom is trying to get a feel for all of us as players and experimenting with different combinations — a smart thing to do. He isn't saying much at the start, just mostly watching. I take nothing for granted. I approach every training session as if I am fighting for a spot on the team, going for my first cap. I don't want anything to determine my fate other than my play.

A friend says to me, "Relax, Carli. Do you think you really have to prove yourself at this point?"

Relaxing isn't in my DNA on the field, especially when there's a new coach on board.

"I don't know what Tom thinks, or what he's been told," I reply. "I'm leaving nothing to chance. I'm going to empty the tank every day."

We head to Portugal for our annual Algarve Cup appearance, and we open against Iceland. About fifteen minutes in, I am shoved from behind and land hard on my left shoulder. I hear a crack. I get right up and keep playing, but I know something is wrong. My arm feels weak and painful. I can't push off with it at all and have to keep it right at my side when I run. I finish the half and get it looked at by a doctor and trainer.

The doctor doesn't think it is serious and says my strength in it is actually quite good.

"You should be able to play with it," he says.

I am heartened by the diagnosis, but I have my doubts. The crack

I heard wasn't from stepping on an acorn. I start the second half and go for almost twenty minutes until the pain gets to be too much. Tom subs me out and brings in Christen Press.

We beat Iceland, 3–0, but it's hard for me to enjoy it. The pain is much worse the next day, after the adrenaline wears off. I ice it and get treatment and am so ticked off this happened, it's making me crazy. I go for a run on a treadmill because I don't want to lose fitness. I do sprints at practice with my left arm dangling like a loose thread, but there's no getting around the facts: I am going to be a spectator for the rest of the Algarve Cup.

The pain persists, keeping me up at night, so I lie in bed and have a movie marathon until dawn. I am hurt, and I am worried. I've been rehabbing and doing everything necessary to feel better, get my strength back, and get back on the field. I'm planning to play in the final, but the doctor wants me to get an MRI and X-ray to make sure nothing serious happened. We get the results immediately, and it isn't good news. The images show a break in the tuberosity bone of my shoulder. Obviously, I'm told I cannot play.

We play Germany in the final and win 2–0, but I am out for six to eight weeks.

I miss a team trip to Germany and the Netherlands as I rehab my shoulder. The only good thing about the forced break is that Brian and I have our longest uninterrupted time together in ages.

The shoulder responds well to rest and rehab, and the eight-week X-ray looks good, so I am cleared to play and head off to Buffalo to join the Western New York Flash, my new team in yet another incarnation of women's pro soccer. This one is called the National Women's Soccer League, and all I can do is hope it gets some traction and outlasts its predecessors, the WUSA and the WPS. Abby, the local kid made good, is the star of the Flash, and it's great to be together. We connect well and win the first two games I play before Abby and I head off to a weeklong national team camp, play solidly in a 3–0 victory over Canada, and then head back to Buffalo, where I score my first goal in front of the home crowd. It's a wacky juggling act, bouncing back and forth between the Flash and the national team, but we know that the league needs the national team players if it's going to have a chance at survival.

You do what you have to do.

One of my other concerns is how I should approach Dawn Scott, our fitness trainer. I totally respect Dawn. She is so committed to her work and has made a huge difference in our team's overall fitness, but she is worried that I am doing too much extra stuff on the side.

"I love your work ethic, but you have to give your body a chance to recharge," she says.

I know rest is important. I also know my body, and know that I need the extra fitness work to be at a world-class level. Heather O'Reilly and Kelley O'Hara have lungs the size of hot-air balloons and can run all day. I can't. The extra work is how I play catch-up.

Dawn is also encouraging me to lift weights, to get stronger and more explosive. Again, I know she is just doing her job, but the fact is that weights may work for other people, but I've found that they just don't give me the results I am looking for.

"Weights make me slow," I tell Dawn. "They make me less agile. I do plenty of strength work using body weight, whether it's push-ups, ropes, TRX, bands, or whatever. I don't mean to be difficult or high-maintenance. I am totally committed to getting stronger, and I've learned this is the best way to do that for me."

Dawn doesn't just hear me; she helps me find body-weight exercises that will achieve the desired result. It's all good. I follow up with Tom and make sure he understands that I am doing everything I need to do to be fit and strong — I am just doing it the way that works best for me.

"You've proven you know what it takes," Tom says. "However you want to do your work is fine."

Our next friendly is back home in Jersey at Red Bull Arena, against South Korea. We're undefeated in ten games under Tom, and though there is some grumbling about his ever-changing lineups, you can't argue with the results. In the tenth minute, Abby gets nice service in the box from Lauren Cheney, settles the ball with her left foot, pivots, and drills a ball in the near side for a 1–0 lead. Eight minutes later, I carry the ball in midfield and flick a pass out wide to the left, and soon Cheney is on the ball again, lofting a cross in front, where Abby delivers — yes — a diving header to make it 2–0. The goal ties Abby with Mia Hamm atop the all-time U.S. scoring list with 158 goals, and the tie does not last for long, because before the game is a half-hour old Abby knocks in another header off a Pinoe corner kick. Now she is alone at number 159, the greatest soccer scorer in American history. I rush toward Abby to hug her, and so does the whole team, our bench players sprinting out onto the field in their green pinnies, the crowd standing and cheering. It is a beautiful moment. Abby and I haven't always been on the same side of things, but I've always admired her love of the game and the indomitable strength and will she brings to the striker position. She loves to score goals and she loves to win, and to her everlasting credit, she loves to share the glory, crediting her teammates for making her look good. Abby has always been that way, and it says a whole lot about her as a person. I am happy for Abby that she breaks the record, and happy again when she scores number four — number 160 overall — in stoppage time of the first half.

As if four goals in a half and setting a cherished record are not enough, Abby also accepts the captain's armband after Christie Rampone is subbed out. When it is Abby's time to come off, Tom and Paul Rogers, his assistant coach, apparently want Abby to hand it to me and are emphatically gesturing to get Abby's attention on the sideline. Though it may seem to be a minor matter in the middle of a blowout victory, it isn't minor to Hope Solo, our star goalkeeper, who is not on the roster as she recovers from surgery.

"It is awesome to see you get the respect you finally deserve," Hope says in a text. "People tried so hard not to like you for whatever reason, jealousy or whatever, but you demanded respect by your commitment to being the best and by your play. And we finally have a staff that has ultimate respect for you and for once you don't have to prove anything to anybody.

"You will always be my captain."

It is one of the most touching messages I've ever gotten.

During another trip back to Jersey to face Sky Blue, I want to keep the positive momentum going with my parents. They tell me they are planning on coming to the game.

"Great, I will leave you tickets," I say. I haven't seen them in four months because of my commitments with the national team and the Flash. My cousins and aunts and uncles and other friends are coming to the game as well. I am just hoping everybody can get along.

"It'll be good to see you," I tell my parents.

My parents bring along my aunt Lorraine, my father's sister. We have a strong game, and I score a goal and am looking forward to visiting with everyone afterwards, especially my parents. They haven't been to one of my games in a long time. They are the people who were there when I was with the Delran Dynamite. My father was the one who always set up his folding chair by the corner flag, to get the best possible view of my attacking game.

When I get to the meeting area, I don't see my parents anywhere. I am puzzled. I hope everything is okay. I ask Brian and my cousin Jaime if they've seen my parents.

"No, I think they left," Jaime says.

"They left? Why would they leave?" I say. I think, *There's no way they would just leave without saying anything to me.*

But I am wrong. They didn't wait. For whatever reason, they left without even saying hello. As Brian and I drive away from the field, my mom sends me a text message: "hi carli, it was great to see you play in person. sorry we didn't see you after the game, we knew you had a lot of people there and didn't want to keep you from seeing them. Love mom and dad." I haven't seen my parents since.

The Flash gets better and better as the season goes on. In a game against Washington, Abby plays great balls to me all night, and it is my turn to fill the net. I score three times in a 4–0 victory. I earn NWSL Player of the Week honors, and we go six weeks without losing a game, securing a playoff spot against Sky Blue, a team we've beaten twice by a 3–0 margin. Jim Gabarra is the Sky Blue coach, and I heard earlier in the year that he has talked crap about me to the Flash owner, telling him I'm going to be a big headache for him — if not now, then soon.

Some people are good at letting things like this go, but I am not one of them. I'm not necessarily proud of that, but it's the way I am. If you diss me or dismiss me, I am going to remember. We beat Sky Blue, 2–0, in the semifinals. I score both goals, the second after a thirty-five-yard run that ends with a rocket into the upper ninety.

I shake Jim Gabarra's hand after the game and say, "Next time maybe you will think twice about saying stuff about me."

He says he doesn't know what I am talking about.

"You know *exactly* what I am talking about," I say, and then I walk away.

We wind up losing the final to Portland, which gets a sick goal from Tobin Heath from about thirty-six yards out. It's not the ending I am looking for, but it's been a good year on the whole, and I return to the national team in strong form. We finish the year undefeated, with a 4–1 victory over Brazil. I have a part in three of the four goals. We seem to be flourishing as we head into 2014 and World Cup qualifying, a side that seems ready to reach a new level and cement its status as the best women's soccer team in the world.

It's too bad it doesn't work out that way.

14

Coaching Carousel Part II

I FEEL STRONGER AND FITTER than I ever have in our first camp of 2014 in Los Angeles. My shooting is off in training and that is annoying, and I am thinking a bit too much on the field, but otherwise I am ready to crush it this year.

The mood teamwide is not as good. We take a three-week swing through Dallas, Fort Lauderdale, and Atlanta, and it doesn't start well in a friendly against Canada. I am sitting it out after getting two yellow cards in our last game against Brazil, so we have some new pieces in new places, and the result isn't up to our usual standard. The first twenty minutes are okay, and we do wind up winning on a goal by Sydney Leroux, but our possession and creativity are lacking. We do a lot of dumping the ball into the box and hoping for the best.

It is not what Tom Sermanni is looking for from the top-ranked team in the world.

We beat up on Russia in two games in February — combined score 15–0 — and head off to Portugal for Algarve, a tournament we've completely dominated, winning three of the last four titles and eight of the last eleven, but we are a side in flux. Abby hasn't been at the top of her game. Tom meets with her and tells her she is behind Press and Leroux right now.

We open against Japan, and Abby is sitting. We have a number of opportunities early but don't convert. I score on a left-footer from the right side early on, but it is called off by an offsides. It's not until the fifty-ninth minute that we finally break through, when Syd runs at the Japanese keeper, gets a piece of the ensuing goal kick, and watches as it trickles into the Japanese goal. It is as bad a gaffe as you will ever see a keeper make, but Syd's hustle made it happen. Aya Miyama ties it in the final seven minutes on a thirty-five-yard free kick that Hope doesn't get a good read on.

Two days later we take on Sweden, coached by our old friend Pia. It is so strange seeing her on the other sideline. Abby is starting because Syd came down with something, and the day doesn't begin well. About fifteen minutes in, Amy Rodriguez gets hauled down in the box and Abby steps up to the spot, but the Swedish keeper makes a diving stop of her PK. Sweden takes the lead not even ten minutes later on a beautiful, lunging header by veteran Lotta Schelin.

We dominate the flow of play and have numerous chances but can't convert anything, including a couple of breakaways that Hedvig Lindahl stuffs us on. The 1–0 loss is our first in forty-three games. It means we have no shot at winning the tournament this year. It means the grumbling about Tom will start to get louder.

Tom is a master strategist with a great feel for the game and very much a laissez-faire approach to things. He isn't big on structure, or planning. I like him and like his effort to make us a more sophisticated and creative team, but right now our results on the field are not what we are accustomed to. Next up is Denmark. We fall behind 3–0 in the first half, the first time in the thirty-year history of the U.S. Women's National Team that has ever happened. We wind up closing to 4–3 in the sixty-eighth minute, after I make a cross of a short run in traffic on the left, and Pinoe finishes it off a deflection. Press and Pinoe narrowly miss tying it up. We wind up losing 5–3, and finish with our worst Algarve result ever — seventh place.

Tom is disgusted, and so are we. He says that our touches were sloppy and our giveaways contributed greatly to the result in this tournament.

After an eighteen-day break when most of us return to our NWSL teams, we reconvene for a twelve-day camp in Denver. There is a weird vibe almost from the time camps begins. On the first day we work on crossing and marking in the box and play small-sided games, none of which we have been doing under Tom. Jill Ellis, the program's technical director and Pia's former assistant, is here to observe and record training sessions. I hear that Dan Flynn and Sunil Gulati are supposed to be coming into camp, another curious development if it's true.

All I know is that the World Cup qualifying starts in six months and we need to start getting better every single day, beginning now. We don't want the same kind of excitement we put ourselves through in 2011, when we had to beat Italy to qualify. If we have any shot at winning the World Cup for the first time since 1999, the work and commitment needs to start here.

Our next game is against China in Commerce City, Colorado, on the first Sunday in April. We play with a new alignment — 4-3-3 as opposed to 4-4-2 — and are much better. We're passing well, making runs off the ball, generating all kinds of threats, finally breaking through when the former Lauren Cheney — now Lauren Holiday — slams in a ball from the top of the box late in the first half. Pinoe curls in a direct kick through heavy traffic in the second half, and we come away with a one-sided 2–0 triumph.

We are in the bus going back to the hotel when a team staffer gets up. "Sunil and Dan want to meet with the team at seven thirty tonight," the guy says.

We gather in the hotel, and soon Sunil and Dan arrive, along with the coaching staff, but not Tom. So now we know why everything has felt so odd.

Tom Sermanni is out of a job, fired not long after losing the only two games he ever lost as head coach of the national team.

Sunil tells us this was not just a kneejerk reaction to what happened in Portugal. He has nothing but admiration for Tom as a person, and even as a coach. Sunil says it basically comes down to a "subjective evaluation of where the team is going.

"It just wasn't working. We think we need to go in a different direction, stylistically, or whatever you want to call it," Sunil says. He says that Jill Ellis will take over on an interim basis.

Several players start to cry after the announcement is made. I feel sick about it. I know we haven't played at our usual level, but I have not seen this coming at all. When Sunil and Dan leave, Tom comes in and speaks to us.

"This unfortunately is part of sport," he says. "I'm thankful for the opportunity to coach you, and thank you all for your effort and hard work. It's been an honor to coach you, and I wish you all the best going forward."

When Sunil, Dan, and Tom are gone, we talk about everything among ourselves. I listen for a while as Lauren, Abby, and Christie talk about it all. Then I have something to say.

"One thing that I think will really help us as a team is to stop bitching when there are issues or we're not happy with something. If an issue needs to be addressed, approach that person. We need to be more up front with each other. We need to stop all the chatter because it's destructive and it's contagious."

Later, I visit Tom in his room.

"How are you holding up?" I ask.

"I'm okay, Carli," he says. "Thank you. You are playing at a very high level, and I hope you keep that up. You are a true professional, and all I can say is, I wish I had twenty players with your attitude."

"I appreciate that, Tom. You've done nothing but give me support. You're handling this in a class way. You're a very good coach, and I know you will land on your feet."

I have a horrible sleep that night. I keep thinking about Tom and all this sudden upheaval so close to World Cup qualifying. Whoever is coaching us, we need to get it together.

We fly to San Diego for our next game, also against China. The night before we all hang out in Jill's room and have s'mores, team-bonding over chocolate, graham crackers, and marshmallows. It's light and fun.

I am totally fired up for this game. I want to start this new era off right, to send a message. We come out flying. I have a great chance in front in the opening ten minutes, but knock it just wide. We keep pushing. Ten minutes later, I one-time a carom off of Holiday and rip it past the keeper to get us going. Three minutes later, I get some space twenty-five yards out and let fly with a lefty dipper that rockets inside the left post. It's my fiftieth career goal, and I find out later that it puts me ninth on the all-time U.S. scoring list. Syd finishes the scoring with an angled left-footer on the ground. When I get Player of the Game, it makes a good day even better.

So the Jill Ellis era is off to a 1–0 start, and continues in May in Winnipeg, Canada — the same city where we will open our World Cup in thirteen months. Jill, officially, is still the interim coach, but I am positive she will get the job. She's well respected, has been around the program a long time, and knows the team as well as anyone. Jill has a series of positional meetings in our Winnipeg hotel and asks to meet with me before our friendly against Canada. We are in Jill's hotel room.

"It's time you stepped up and took a leadership role on this team," she says. "You have earned your stripes. You've won gold medals. You've scored in the biggest games. You have earned the respect of everyone with the way you work and your commitment to the team, and now it's time for you to put the team on your shoulders and win the World Cup. No matter who is coaching this team, you need to do this."

I sit and take in what Jill is saying. I don't say anything at first. It's as big a vote of confidence as I have ever gotten from a coach. I liked Jill from the first time I met her when she coached the U-21 team. She is someone who sees the positives in a situation and then works at fixing the things that aren't positive.

I thank her for her faith and agree that it's time for me to be more out front in how I lead.

"I am ready to do whatever it takes — *whatever it takes* — to bring the World Cup back to the United States," I tell her.

Supported by a big and enthusiastic home crowd, the Canadians take a 1–0 lead. We are not at our best, but we are fighting hard. Abby gets robbed by Canadian keeper Erin McLeod, a little payback for the whole one-two-three counting gambit in the 2012 Olympics. I run a give-and-go with Abby that leads to a cross in front to Heather O'Reilly, but her shot caroms just wide. Syd scores a late goal with a timely finish off a defensive misplay, and we get away with a 1–1 tie.

A week later, U.S. Soccer makes it official: Jill Ellis is the eighth coach of the U.S. Women's National Team. I am thrilled for her and thrilled for our team because I know that Jill is the perfect fit for us. She's smart, knowledgeable, and experienced, and though she is friendly and approachable, she is nobody's pushover.

I text her as soon as I hear: "Congrats on the job! Real happy you got it now let's go start the road to winning the World Cup."

Jill replies:

"Heck, yeah. So dang excited. I cannot wait to see you in Tampa. ☺ "

Tampa comes around in a couple of weeks, Jill's first camp as head coach. There's an infusion of energy and enthusiasm, and though we don't play our best game, we defeat a strong French team, 1–0. We then have a return engagement in East Hartford, Connecticut, five days later. Jill names me captain for the game and tells me again that she wants me to be a leader and to be more vocal. Tony Gustavsson, a Swede who Jill just named as her top assistant, meets with me before the game. He shows me clips from the first France game and says the team needs me to push higher up on the field and impact the game more by using my attacking skills.

"You can win games for this team, and we need to get you into a position to do that," Tony says.

"I want to attack. I love to attack," I tell him. "And I totally agree that I can help the team even more by pushing higher."

We play France to a 2–2 tie, and I feel much more active and impactful in the middle of the field. I have worked my butt off for years for every coach I've ever had, but I can't deny that I feel a special connection with Jill. We have very different backgrounds — she grew up in England and didn't start playing soccer until the family moved to Virginia when she was a teenager — but in so many ways we are the same person. I am, at my core, an introvert, and so is Jill. I just want to be with my people, and so does Jill. Neither of us wants to be fussed over, and we're both completely transparent. All this does is make me want to play even harder for her. Jill Ellis is one of the most authentic people I've ever met. I love that about her. I think she is going to do great things with this team.

Something has been bugging me for a while with the Western New York Flash. I try to deny it at first, but I can't anymore, because it's getting out of hand. I have a teammate — yes, someone on my own side — who goes out of her way to hit me in training sessions. At first I think that maybe it is accidental. It is not accidental. She is gunning for me, and has been since the preseason. She is my own teammate, and she is absolutely trying to wipe me out, tackling me in training or scrimmages with red-card intensity. I don't know what her problem is. Maybe it's because I am a national team player and she isn't. I don't really care, honestly.

It is time for it to stop.

We're near the end of a training session, playing 6 v. 6. There's a ball in the air. My "teammate" is ready to play it, not far from me. I see what is unfolding. It is the perfect time. I run toward her and go up for the ball. I get the ball — and plenty of her too. She goes flying and then crashes to the ground.

Everybody is speechless, not believing what just happened.

She isn't hurt, just shaken. Which is exactly what I want. I don't want to hurt anybody, ever. I just want her to know I am not going to stand for her trying to hunt me down anymore.

She looks at me incredulously, as if to say, *How could you do that to your teammate?*

We never exchange a word about what happened, before, during, or after. I am not sorry. This needed to be done. Not only does she never try to wipe me out again, but we get along better than ever after that.

· · ·

The whole year has been pointing toward World Cup qualifying, and it is finally here, with an opening game against Trinidad and Tobago in Kansas City. I am in the attacking third a lot, and we are creating all sorts of chances but don't break through until the fifty-fifth minute, when I play a through ball to Alex Morgan, who cuts left and crosses to Abby, who heads it in. That lone goal holds up. We then move on to Chicago, where we take apart Guatemala, 5–0, before moving on to Washington, D.C., for a CONCACAF semifinal against Haiti. Jill and Tony talk beforehand about scoring early in this game to assert our dominance, and I oblige, chesting a punchout from the Haitian keeper to the ground, then half-volleying a shot into the corner to make it 1–0. Abby scores twice, and the onslaught is on, the final score running to 6–0 and setting us up with a date against Mexico in Chester, Pennsylvania. The winner will advance to the World Cup.

It is my first game back in this stadium since the game against China before the 2012 Olympics when I lost my starting spot. It is also a prime chance to pay back Mexico for beating us in qualifying four years earlier. These things may not seem like a big deal, but when you play so many games, over so many years, these extra layers of motivation are important. I want to crush it in Chester. I want to crush Mexico. I want to expunge every bit of the unsavory memories I have of both, so it is straight from my script when Tobin Heath lofts a beautiful cross early on. I am in front, unmarked, and head it into the goal. I follow with a PK goal after Tobin is dragged down in the box. We win 3–0.

We are going to the World Cup in Canada.

I wish we could start playing today.

15

Character Builders

JILL ELLIS HAS A PLAN, and nobody much likes it. She schedules a long, four-game trip to Brasilia, Brazil, one apiece against
China and Argentina and two against Brazil, right before the end of
the year. Jill has her reasons.

"I just felt this team needed some adversity, to face some hard
challenges," Jill says. "And this trip had a lot of them. It was challenging logistically. The fields were bad. Everything was complicated. We
were literally in our off-season, and now I am bringing them halfway
across the world. I wanted them to be booed by eighteen thousand
people. I wanted them to play a team that was going to challenge us. I
told them, 'You're expanding your comfort level by being uncomfortable and that is going to pay dividends down the road because now
when a curveball is thrown at you, you're going to be able to hit it out
of the park because you've shown the ability to adjust.'"

We do not hit much of anything out of the park in Brasilia. Mostly,
we hit broken-bat singles. We open against China, and we are not
sharp at all. As a team, we are coming off of a six-week break; our
fitness level isn't very high, and we're not possessing the ball well. I
flick in a low, hard cross from Pinoe to make it 1–0 midway through
the first half, but the rest of the game is marked mostly by missed
chances and low-energy play. I am unhappy with both my game and
our collective effort. China scores in the second half for a 1–1 finish.

We know we need to do much better against Brazil a couple of days later.

Things start auspiciously. I score on a spinning left-footer in front in the sixth minute, and when Pinoe follows with a drive from the right into the side of the net, we are up 2–0 not even twenty-five minutes in. We have many other opportunities to add to the lead, but we don't capitalize, and at the other end we are giving Brazil way too much space. We are not applying high pressure, letting Brazil come samba-dancing out of its own end. Marta scores on a beautiful through ball, then scores again on a deft, angled left-footer. In the sixty-fifth minute, she breaks the 2–2 tie by beating Hope on the near side with a shot from distance. It's a ball Hope saves forty-nine times out of fifty, but this one gets past her, and now we have to play catch-up. We do not catch up. We aren't playing quickly enough, our defensive shape is lacking, and the midfield and defense are too far apart. The crowd roars when the match ends and we trudge off, without a victory in two games.

After an off day, we demolish Argentina, 7–0, behind four goals from Press and three from me, but the real test will come when we face Brazil in the final, four days before Christmas.

After the coaches make it clear that we are not going to give the Brazilians the space they had in the first game, we respond by giving them no space at all. We have already heard Marta's name far too much over the PA system. We pretty much park the proverbial bus and sit back in our end, and the Brazilians can't break through. We open it up a bit in the second half. Becky Sauerbrunn knocks a beautiful header that the Brazilian keeper punches into the crossbar. I score on a left-foot shot in front off a cross that is nullified by an offsides call. The game finishes in a scoreless tie.

Though we are better and more organized, we're not even close to where we need to be. If Jill wants us to be uncomfortable, the trip to Brasilia can only be seen as a major success.

At this point, all I want is to be home, to be with Brian, and to get back training with James. I need to reconnect and recharge. Two days after I am back in Jersey, I am in the Blue Barn, doing repeat sprints and working on shooting. On Christmas Eve, I run seventy-five minutes and do some upper-body work and already feel way better than I did in Brazil. It feels good to push myself hard. I can't let up. There's a World Cup in six months. The prep work starts now, even on Christmas Day.

Christmas is my favorite holiday. It has been since I was a little girl. We would always go get the tree together; sometimes we'd even chop one down. We'd decorate it with lights and ornaments, including my favorite—a little globe with a baby inside it. I don't know why I liked that one so much. Maybe the innocence, the purity of it. Christmas felt magical every single year.

On the night before Christmas, we'd all be together as a family —cousins and aunts and uncles, usually at Aunt Patti's house—and then we'd go back to our house and open our presents on Christmas morning. My parents would separate the gifts into piles, one each for Stephen, Ashley, and me. It felt different from every other day of the year. I loved that it was cold out and that everybody was happy. That was the best part. This is the seventh Christmas I've spent apart from my family. It's always a little sad for me to think about that. One day I hope we can celebrate Christmas together again.

We spend that Christmas Day 2014 at Brian's sister Lisa's house, but before we go I head out to Laurel Acres and train, running sprints up the hill. Nobody else is in the park. It's a great, energizing workout. I always train on Christmas Day. For me, it's an affirmation of how committed I am, how I am ready to go even on the most special holiday of the year.

I train right through the New Year. Our camp starts on January 5, and when departure day nears, it's never a fun time. Brian and I have gotten very good at saying good-bye because we have had way too much practice, but the closer we get the more difficult the good-byes get.

"You know, one of these days we will actually be together and not have to do this all the time," I tell him.

Three days before I am to head out to Los Angeles, Brian suggests that we have a belated anniversary celebration of the day we started going together (December 20, 2000). He wants to drive to a charming little enclave in Bucks County, Pennsylvania, called Peddler's Village, a cluster of antique stone buildings and nice shops, done up beautifully with lights and decorations for the holidays. We're going to stroll through the cobblestone streets and do some exploring and then have a quiet dinner at a place called the Yardley Inn.

It's a Friday night, and as we walk through Peddler's Village, Brian is unusually quiet. He seems preoccupied. I hope nothing is wrong. I don't know what's going on. I decide to let it go.

"You want to have a cup of hot chocolate?" he says.

"Sure," I reply.

We stop at a café, and Brian looks around for an empty table. There are none — and that seems to annoy him. We stroll with our hot chocolate, and then Brian suggests we walk over to a gazebo, which is normally a private sort of place but at the moment is full of gingerbread houses and people looking at the gingerbread houses. We keep walking. I am on Brian's right, before he suddenly circles around to the other side of me. Now I am on his left.

Brian is definitely not himself, I think.

Through the quaint streets of Peddler's Village we go, until we come upon a tunnel decorated with little white Christmas lights that are twinkling all around us. Brian stops in the tunnel.

"Let's take a picture," he says, holding out his phone at arm's length.

Brian never wants to take selfies. I wish I knew what was up with him.

And then, a moment or two after he puts his phone away, Brian Hollins falls to one knee, right in the middle of the tunnel. He reaches for my hand.

"I've been waiting to do this for a very long time," he says. "Carli, you are the love of my life, and I want to spend the rest of my life with you. Will you marry me?"

I start to tear up before I can even say yes. Brian waits for a herd of people in the tunnel to go by and then reaches into his inside coat pocket and pulls out a small box. He hands it to me, and I open it up. It is the most beautiful engagement ring I have ever seen. I slip it on, and it fits perfectly. Now Brian and I, future husband and wife, are wrapped in each other's arms under the twinkling white lights, and it doesn't matter who else is in the tunnel.

It is the happiest moment of my life.

A little later, in the Yardley Inn, we are both so excited we can barely eat. Brian explains all of the little oddities I kept noticing, and now they all make sense. He didn't want me walking near the pocket where he had the ring for fear that I might discover it — hence the end-around. He was thinking of proposing over hot chocolate, but it was too crowded and there was no private place to sit. His number-one choice was the gazebo, but it was overrun by gingerbread activity and a long line of people. The last resort was the sweet, white-lit tunnel. It is January 2, 2015, and it is the best place to get engaged that I can imagine. I can't wait to share the news with the people we love.

The more I am around Jill, the more I like her. She believes that if we are going to be the best, we have to play the best. There's no sense in going into the World Cup with a series of 5–0 victories behind us that make everybody feel good but are as useful as a flat tire for our preparation. So after a hard four-week camp in Los Angeles in January, she wants to test us in a big way, to have iron sharpen iron.

"One of the first things I did when I got hired was to tell people, 'We haven't won the World Cup in sixteen years,'" Jill says. "'If we want to change that, we can't continue what we've been doing.' That's not a knock on the previous coaches. Not at all. It's just finding ways to create challenges and build a stronger team. I told them I wanted to play the top five teams in the world if we can — boom, boom, boom, boom, boom. We've never done that before, five or six months out from a major world event. We've never played a series of games against the best. Maybe we've played one or two, but that is not enough. I wanted us to go into the World Cup hungry and humbled and understanding that to win it's going to require us paying close attention to all the details — game management, set pieces, things like that."

So the start of our World Cup year begins with games against France and England before we head to Portugal for the Algarve Cup. The only top team Jill can't get scheduled is Germany, just because our available dates don't match up.

Jill is determined to keep stretching our comfort zone as if it were Spandex, and she is no less determined to tighten us and organize us defensively. Pia and Tom both were more inclined to give us room to figure things out and solve problems on our own. They encouraged us to possess the ball and build up through the midfield and create scoring chances that way. It's not that Jill doesn't want us to do that; she just wants to lay down a more disciplined, structured defensive foundation — a system in which we are defending as a unit and staying organized and building out from there.

It is a sound plan, and it needs to be, because we are playing without Hope, who has been suspended by U.S. Soccer in the wake of an incident in which her husband, Jerramy Stevens, is arrested for driving a team van while under the influence. I don't know the details, but I do know it's not an easy spot for Ashlyn Harris, our backup, who will be in the net against the number-three team in the world.

The game against France is every bit the test Jill wants it to be. We have multiple chances to score. I have a great one inside the box, but sky it over the crossbar. Abby gets stuffed on a penalty kick. We never break through, and the French score twice. The 2–0 defeat is the first time we have ever lost to them.

The most disconcerting thing for me is where I am on the field. Jill starts me at left mid, telling me that she wants me to pinch in toward the middle, thinking that being in the wide position may help me get forward faster, which is what she wants. I understand her thinking, and I know she wants to give Lauren Holiday and Morgan Brian a look in the middle of our 4-4-2 alignment, but the truth is, I don't think it works on the field. Holiday is in the middle for the first sixty minutes, and then Jill moves me there. There are immediate payoffs: I feel much more involved in the attack, and I am winning balls and starting counters. The middle is where I want to be. I believe it is where I need to be, for the good of the team.

Jill sticks with the same alignment, with me out wide at left mid, in our next game against England, and though we score a 1–0 victory on a goal by Alex Morgan, I am frustrated by the way I play — and where I play. I miss a great chance to score on a volley, which is all the more maddening because I'd taken about 200 of them with James the week before. I talk to James, and I agree with his assessment that I am not mentally preparing myself to play — not spending enough time visualizing the game and how I want to play.

"You will always play better when you've already visualized the game in your head," says James, who also tells me not to get worked up about the position issue.

"Embrace the change that Jill is making. Be a good soldier. Learn something from it. You are seeing the field from a different perspective. It will make you a stronger player when you are back in the middle."

For now, though, I am still on the left, pinched in, and fixed on erasing the memory of the Algarve debacle of a year earlier — the seventh-place finish that basically cost Tom Sermanni his job. It's important that we make a statement this time around, start putting pieces together. We open up against Norway and fall behind by a goal on a header right before halftime. We apply more pressure in the second half, and ten minutes in I spin on a ball just outside the box and drive a left-footed shot inside the far post to tie the game. I convert a PK off a hand ball in the box six minutes later, and we make the lead hold up. Then we move on to beat Switzerland, 3–0, in a bruising and mostly artless game.

Assured of a place in the final, Jill rests several starters (me included, for the first half) in a scoreless tie game with Iceland. To me, we are playing too cautiously, still parking the bus, and I honestly think it goes back to the losses to Brazil in December and France in February. We have taken on a distinctly defensive posture and are mostly looking to score on counterattacks. I understand that an organized, first-rate defense is vital, but I also believe we're way too good just to absorb pressure and then bust out on the counter. I want to take it to the other team. I want to come at our opponents and see if they can stop us.

We have a rematch against France in the Algarve final. Hope is back from her suspension, so that's a huge lift. Julie Johnston scores on a well-aimed header on Holiday's perfectly placed direct kick, and then Christen Press slices through the spine of the French defense to give us a two-goal lead. Hope stops a PK and is awesome, and we come off with a 2–0 victory, sweet Portuguese payback.

Even though Jill and the staff are ecstatic with the win, I have a different take. It was a strong defensive game, no doubt, but we continue to sit back and play passively, as if we're afraid that if we push numbers forward we're going to leave ourselves vulnerable. We sustain almost no attack against France and have few good chances. I feel largely uninvolved and barely even touch the ball. Of course I am happy with the result, but the manner in which we achieve it is troubling, not because everything must revolve around me but because we're honestly not playing at a high level. Sometimes scores can fool you; they can mask an underlying issue. When I get back to my room, I write in my journal:

We have a long way to go to win the World Cup.

After a twelve-day break, we return to camp in L.A., and one day we scrimmage with a boys' team. I am not happy with how we play. I am out wide on the left, and Holiday and Brian are in the middle. I feel almost useless, like a fifth wheel. Jill walks up to me after the scrimmage. For maybe the first time in my life, I break down on the field. Even I am shocked at the depth of my emotions in that moment.

"What's wrong, Carli?" Jill asks.

I can barely get any words out I am so frustrated. Jill looks at me and says, "Let's meet later." I nod and wipe the tears away and get it together. Later that night, about 9:00 PM, Jill texts me.

"What are you doing?" she says.

"I'm in my PJs, getting ready for bed," I reply.

"I'm in my PJs too. Why don't you come up to my room for a few minutes and we'll talk."

When I get to Jill's room, her daughter, Lily, is asleep in the other bed. I start talking about this left-mid experiment and how I think it is not working for anybody. I am not alone in this opinion either. Abby, for one, is telling me constantly that the team needs me in the middle of the field. Others are saying the same thing. I'm not looking to be insubordinate but rather to openly voice an opinion about the direction of the team.

"I respect you totally and will do whatever it takes and whatever you want, but that's how I feel," I tell Jill. And then, suddenly, I break down again, emotions sweeping over me in tidal waves, my voice shaky and cracking.

"I'm so frustrated. I just want to help us win," I say.

"It's okay, Carli. It's okay," Jill says. She listens to everything I have to say and tells me that she's glad I am being honest with my emotions. She has a kind and comforting way about her.

"I know you want what's best for the team. You have always been team-oriented, from the first time I coached you," Jill says. "Listen, we just wanted to try some things. It's a process we have to go through, and sometimes there are struggles when people are in different roles. I've watched these games and spoken with the other coaches, and everybody seems to agree that we need you back in the middle. You did very well outside, but it's not the same when we don't have you attacking and distributing and tackling in the middle of the field.

"We're going to be better for having gone through this, and so will you, I think. But don't you worry. You will be back in the eight."

Eight is the number soccer coaches use to refer to a traditional center midfielder. Eight is where I want to be. It is a great pajama talk. I go back to my room feeling much better about things.

We travel to St. Louis to play New Zealand on April 4, one day before the Cardinals open their season in Busch Stadium. More than 35,000 people turn out, the biggest crowd for a stand-alone friendly we've ever had. I feel short on confidence as the game begins,

weighted by pressure to prove to Jill I was right. The best antidote to
that is to play simply, to get into the flow of things, to help with the
buildup.

That is exactly what I do.

I am taking few touches, moving the ball around, getting people
linked up. Just five minutes in I play a ball back, and it swings wide
to the left, where Meghan Klingenberg is overlapping. I see space
in front of me and make a run into the box, and Kling finds me perfectly. I carry the ball in and flick a centering pass as Amy Rodriguez
and Christen Press crash the goal. The ball is deflected away, but it
is a strong offensive thrust by us. I am heartened, no matter that we
didn't score. This is how I want us to play.

Kling hits a blistering shot from outside the box to open the scoring, and we add three more late goals in a six-minute span for a 4–0
victory. It is the best game we've played in a while, and the most grat-
ifying game I've played in a while. I take care of the ball well in the
middle and tackle relentlessly, and our strong pushes up the middle
all game open up the flanks for us.

The World Cup is two months out, and it's crucial to keep building toward a peak. We have three more friendlies left, and it's time to
do all the fine-tuning we can, to work on all the details that Jill says
could well make the difference in Canada.

More than that, it is a time to regain our defiance and swagger, our
drive to do whatever it takes to win a ball, make a stop, make the difference.

We take care of Ireland, 3–0, on Mother's Day, getting two goals
from Abby, which is a great sign. Abby doesn't get the minutes she
used to, but she is still a goal-scoring dynamo, a proven difference-
maker. Having her confident and in a good place going into the
World Cup is huge, even more so with Alex Morgan out with a bone
bruise she suffered against New Zealand. Abby gets set up by Press
on a cross for the first goal. Then I get the ball on the left end line, cut
a defender, and hit a little chip in front that Abby heads in for number two.

Abby buries two more goals in a 5–1 rout of Mexico a week later, getting the second on a sensational cross from Tobin Heath, who fakes her Mexican mark halfway to Guadalajara and lofts a ball that Abby knows just what to do with. Sydney Leroux scores twice as well, her best game of the year, and from start to finish we are firing at Mexico from near and far. Feeling superfit and confident, I return home for one last break before the World Cup. I take hundreds of shots and run the hill at Laurel Acres and do intervals on the track, grinding out rep after rep with James watching. I feel explosive, and I want to be even more explosive. I want to be able to take two steps toward a loose ball and leave everybody in my rearview mirror. This isn't training for the sake of training; it's training with a purpose.

It's training to win a World Cup.

"You are going to have something left in the tank when everybody else's is empty," James tells me.

Our send-off game before the World Cup is right at home, in Red Bull Arena in Harrison, New Jersey, against South Korea. Brian is there, and so are Karen and Kathy, my cousin Jaime, and others. My parents and siblings are not there. There has been no contact. It's not something I can focus on right now. I want to crush it in this game. I want the perfect farewell before we head to Winnipeg, Canada, for the biggest soccer tournament of my life. I want this to be a big Jersey day all around.

Our performance as a team in a 0–0 draw is well short of our best, and the media pretty much buries us for not pounding South Korea. While our approach was more direct, if less effective, than it has been recently, I am trying not to be worried about it.

Who gets all worked up about the last game of spring training?

No, it is not a vintage U.S. game, but negativity is like quicksand; you hang around it enough and it will take you all the way down and you will never be heard from again. I am hard enough on myself that I can make my own negativity, so I really don't need any help.

I am named the Player of the Match against South Korea, and though we didn't get our desired result, I will take it. I am fitter than

I have ever been. I have been training for this for years and feel more ready for this tournament than any other tournament I have ever played in in my life.

We take a charter flight to Winnipeg, Canada. It is June 2015, and my third World Cup is days away. Neither of the first two went anything close to the way I had hoped.

It is time to change the narrative.

16

Disappearing Act

I AM LOOKING AT MYSELF on a computer screen, and the images aren't pretty. I am in our team meeting room in our Winnipeg hotel, sitting at a long folding table, flanked by Jill Ellis on one side and her assistants, Tony Gustavsson and Steve Swanson, on the other. It is the day before we open our World Cup against Australia, and Jill and Steve want to show me video clips of various fouls I've committed in some of our recent games. Most were for coming in from behind, or for putting a little too much crunch into my tackles. One of them came in the first half against Mexico just a few weeks earlier, when I went in late and hard on a sliding tackle a couple of seconds after I got whacked; there was no call.

I got whistled for a foul but didn't get a card, even though I could have.

The point of the video review is to caution me about excessive aggression. Of course they want me to be physical and make crunching tackles, but they also want to remind me that two yellows in the World Cup group stage means you sit for a game.

"We just need you to be careful," Jill says. "We don't want you to change your game. We want you to make good tackles and win possession for us. Just don't go overboard with it — maybe throttle it back a bit, especially when you are coming in from behind."

I get it.

"Believe me, the last thing I want is to miss a World Cup game," I assure them. "I'll be careful."

I file a mental note about it and go for a walk in downtown Winnipeg. I sit by the edge of a fountain. The sound of the flowing water is soothing. I start to write in my journal. I have been keeping a journal since I first made the national team in 2006. Besides being therapeutic, it gives me an in-the-moment record of my thoughts and feelings, successes and stresses; it's a competitive and emotional archive. This day's entry focuses on the great place I am in mentally, the supreme self-belief that comes when you feel that you are truly a better player than you have ever been.

I have never been more ready to play. I am relieved to know that Brian, Jaime, my aunt Patti, and everybody else knows not to come to Canada. I debate once again whether it seems harsh to not share this experience with my fiancé, but come to the same conclusion: I know how I am—if Brian were here, I'd be thinking about him and wanting to be sure he was okay. I had family at my two previous World Cups, and given the outcomes, I do not want to go for the hat trick.

I am rooming with Hope, who always has the TV on to check out games in other groups from all over Canada. I don't want to watch one second. I just want to play. That's it. I am completely in a mental bunker.

Day breaks sunny and warm on June 8, 2015. I sleep well and have eggs, yogurt, and fruit — my usual pregame meal. Once breakfast settles, I head out for my fifteen-minute game-day run from our hotel, down St. Mary Avenue in downtown Winnipeg, past streets named Hargrave and Donald and Smith, toward the Red River. When my watch hits seven and a half minutes, I turn around and head back. I stretch and hydrate and shower, then have a light lunch — salad and fruit. I never eat anything heavy on game days. I want to feel light, hungry.

Outside our hotel we pass through a gauntlet of fans who cheer as we board the bus for the short ride to the University of Manitoba. I head for my seat in the back, cue up "Dreamer" on my iPod, and re-read the email James has sent. Jill gathers us together before we head out and goes over some last-second strategic reminders.

The stadium is packed, and it's so loud and overwhelmingly pro-American that we might as well be back in the States.

Sitting quietly in the locker room moments before our walkout, I am feeling oddly out of sorts. My legs are leaden.

You'll feel better when you get out there and start running, I tell myself.

Australia kicks off and applies pressure almost immediately. In the fifth minute, Australian Emily van Egmond blasts a shot that Hope stops with a diving punchout. Moments later, I touch the ball for only the second time in the game and give it away deep in our end. No harm comes of it, but I am sick that I did that.

You are better than that. This is the World Cup you've been waiting for years for. C'mon, Carli. Raise your game, I tell myself.

The game continues. We are playing poorly, losing possession, knocking random long balls up the field. I don't complete my first pass until the ninth minute. I make a clean, strong tackle for a take-away and hope that it is something to build on and get me into the game.

It is not.

I don't feel like myself. I feel passive. The leaden sensation never lifts. I can't stop thinking of the film session with Jill and her assis-tants, and I can feel myself backing off too much, almost becoming a bystander. Going in hard on tackles isn't just a trademark of mine. It's a part of my game plan. I always make a point to have a crunch-ing tackle early in a game. Not to be dirty or to cheap-shot anybody. Just to let my opponents know what they are going to be up against when they are pressing the attack in the midfield. It's another item from the James playbook: crunching tackles early can set the tone for an entire game, the same way a baseball pitcher might come up and in on a hot hitter in his first at-bat.

But against Australia I am not crunching. I am barely even tapping. It's all so weird. I am just not myself, and we as a team are not ourselves either. Pinoe scores on a deflected strike, and that's about the only good thing I can say about the first half, which ends with us tied at one, even though we've been outplayed throughout. We have our savior in red — Hope Solo — to thank for that. After the early stop on van Egmond, she turned away two more dangerous chances that easily could've left us looking at a two-goal deficit at the half.

Jill has made it clear throughout the run-up to the World Cup that we don't want to peak too early. It is, after all, a monthlong tournament.

"I am not looking for us to play our best game against Australia," she said.

She need not have worried.

We are playing defensively, allowing Australia to dominate possession. Lauren Holiday and I, the center mids, are under instruction to play as number sixes — or holding midfielders — and play the ball out wide. We're not connecting with the forward line, threading through balls, or changing fields. It feels as if we're stuck in neutral for almost all of the ninety minutes. Australia is a solid and improving side, but the Aussies have never beaten us. You never would've guessed that watching the first half.

I feel horrible in the locker room at halftime, low in energy and spirit.

The second half starts better when I make a good strip in the opening two minutes, but then I have too much weight on my pass and it rolls out of bounds. On and on it goes for me. I make a promising run after delivering a pass, but it misses the mark and goes the other way. We raise our game enough to take a 3–1 victory on second-half goals by Press and another one from Pinoe, but we can't let ourselves be fooled by the final score. It was a sloppy effort almost from start to finish, and Hope bailed us out.

My number-one objective going into our second group game — against Pia Sundhage and Sweden — is to wipe out my mental hard-drive and reboot. There is nothing else to do. I resolve to start now, to join the battle in our second game and bring all I've got.

"In the grand scheme of things, nobody is going to remember much about who did what in the first game of the World Cup," James reminds me.

Before I even get to game day, though, another unscripted chapter unfolds. In an interview published in the *New York Times,* Pia makes some sharply critical comments about me and several others, notably Hope and Abby.

"Carli Lloyd was a challenge to coach," Pia tells the *Times.* "When she felt that we had faith in her, she could be one of the best players. But if she began to question that faith, she could be one of the worst.

"It was so delicate, so, so delicate."

Apart from Pia being wrong — if I am so delicate, how did I come back from being benched to score both goals to win Pia her second Olympic gold medal? — I feel completely betrayed. I played my heart out for her. I helped her build an international reputation. I was completely loyal to her, even when others were trying to push her out.

This is my thanks?

I tell the press that Pia is way off base, and I will prove it on the field. It is a good answer, a classy answer. The only problem is that in our second World Cup game I do not prove anything on the field.

I spend most of the ninety minutes trying to be perfect instead of just playing. I am not attacking, not taking risks, and playing with a strange reticence, like a swimmer who dips her toe in the pool but is afraid to dive in. Most of our team seems similarly afflicted, and with Sweden staying compact and organized in its end, our chances are few.

The highlight for me is when I play a good ball forward to Press, who plays it off to Pinoe, who threads it back to me as I make a run on the left side. My leaning, left-footed strike is batted over the crossbar by the Swedish keeper Hedvig Lindahl, and the game remains scoreless. It's a quality save, but not nearly as good as Meghan Klingenberg's. Standing on the goal line during a scramble off a corner kick, Kling watches Sweden's Caroline Seger artfully flick a ball with the outside of her right foot toward our goal. Hope is out of the play, and it seems to be a lock to go in, but then five-feet, two-inch Kling jumps as high as she can go, heading the ball into the crossbar and safely away. The game ends 0–0.

Though we are atop Group D, you would never know it by the way we are getting ripped for our listless, unimaginative play, especially on the offensive end. Our back line and Hope have been superb, and somehow that is what we have morphed into, a defense-first side that doesn't want to commit numbers on the attack and is displaying a lack of patience and skill when we do attack.

After the game, when Jill asks Holiday and me to meet with her, the topic is all about our defensive angles and how we can't let ourselves get split when we defending.

I walk out of that meeting feeling even worse.

I am not even defending the right way, I think.

We fly west to Vancouver for our third Group D game, against Nigeria, a dangerous, physically gifted team that put up three goals on Sweden. My mental demons are running amok as the game approaches. I feel as if I've let the team down, myself down, and James down. How could someone who a mere week ago was poised to have the tournament of her life suddenly turn into an MIA midfielder with a number 10 on her back?

Knowing I'm not in a good frame of mind, Hope invites me to join her and her husband Jerramy for lunch and then for a drive into the mountains. We ride on a gondola, and the majesty of the Canadian Rockies is breathtaking. It takes me to a different mental place, turns off that endless self-critical loop for a while. Afterwards, we take in a lumberjack show, an attraction that I don't run across too often in South Jersey. There's ax-throwing and logrolling and crosscut sawing, beefy men in red flannel shirts everywhere you look. I'm not contemplating a career change, but it's cool to see people who are really into what they do.

Back down at sea level, the biggest challenge facing me isn't how I am playing. It is how I am thinking. I have almost no clarity. I am judging myself without mercy. I am in danger of wallowing my way right out of the World Cup. About the only thing I feel sure about is that if there is anyone who can help quiet the noise in my head, it is my trainer of twelve years.

James Galanis.

So we talk. James reminds me that Nigeria represents another opportunity for a fresh start, and he has a good idea of how to make the most of it.

"Start small when you go out there," he says. "Don't take big risks or play long through balls in the beginning. Keep it simple. Focus on having a clean touch and making a clean pass. Once you start to feel better and your confidence improves, then you start doing more involved things. The important thing is to create some success, build up a nice body of work over the first half, say, and let's see where we go from there."

On a designed play off the opening kickoff, I ping a fifty-yard ball on target to Abby's head, and it almost results in a goal in the first twenty seconds. It's as good a ball as I've played in three games, an encouraging way to start. James's plan seems to be working. I am easing into things, resisting the urge to do too much, taking better care of the ball, not fretting so much about making mistakes. In the fourteenth minute, I yank an open left-footed shot from distance way wide, not a good strike at all, but I don't get down on myself, and a few minutes later I send a perfect twenty-yard ball on the ground up the middle for Alex to run onto.

Jill still has me deeper in the midfield than I'd prefer, but Holiday and I are a bit more involved, and we're starting to combine on a few things offensively. I just miss converting a sliding chance off of a set piece by the left post late in the half, before Abby pounds in a corner kick in the forty-fifth minute to give us a lead. The half is far from a masterpiece, but it's the best we've played so far.

Keep playing simply, let the game come to you, I tell myself at the half.

In the fifty-seventh minute, Pinoe has the ball on the right side and plays a nice square ball for me about five yards outside the box. I have space, and I am about to run onto it and bury it when the ball clips the referee's foot. It never reaches me. I fling up my arms in frustration and run back to defend. I wonder what else could possibly go haywire in this tournament.

We advance to the knockout round with a 1–0 victory, but I can't escape the feeling that, even with a slight upgrade against Nigeria, my World Cup has been an abject disaster and the U.S. is advancing, not because of me, but in spite of me.

Is that an overreaction? No doubt it is. The problem again is my level of expectation, my quest for perfection. It skews everything. When it flares up, it robs me of joy.

Jill reassures me again that it will be fine and that even top players go through these rough patches. The next day she and Michelle French, an assistant coach, show me clips of the Nigeria game, highlighting opportunities I had to change the pace of things and play a greater variety of passes, the way I do when I am right. Switching fields and knocking accurate, long-range passes are two of my strengths. Now I am playing as if the ball is covered with poison ivy and I just want to get it away from me.

We fly to Edmonton to get ready to play Colombia five days later. Our hotel is near a shopping mall, and on an off day James all but orders me to do some retail therapy.

"Don't train. Don't work out. Don't even think about soccer," James says. "Give yourself a break."

I hit Banana Republic and J. Crew and a few other stores, picking up a few things. It's not as mind-clearing as the gondola and the lumberjacks, but at least I stop overanalyzing everything for a while. The day off is good. I go back to work and concentrate on all the basics — my first touches, the weight of my passes, my shooting mechanics — and being aware of all the options that are out there for me on the field. Seeing those film clips with Jill and Frenchie helps. I need to get back to my attacking mentality.

I am tired of playing it safe.

Do not underestimate the power of a single goal. Even a goal that comes from the penalty spot. In the sixty-sixth minute of our game against Colombia, we are holding a 1–0 lead in an unexpectedly tight game when Pinoe gets dragged down in the box after making a strong run off a well-placed pass from Kling. The whistle blows. The referee points to the spot, our second PK opportunity in seventeen minutes. Abby took the first one, after the Colombia keeper was red-carded for tripping Alex in the penalty area. She took it left-footed. She knocked it wide.

Abby looks at me and nods. She is our number-one PK taker, and I am number two. I look back at her. Her message is clear: *This one is yours.*

"Are you sure?" I ask.

She nods again.

I step up and put the ball on the spot. I walk back a half-dozen steps or so and wait for the whistle. I typically prepare for a PK the night before, visualizing how I am going to approach it. Sometimes I might change it up if I see something in the keeper's positioning or her approach (sorry, I am not sharing any state secrets about the variables involved). More often I stick with my plan. This time I calmly drill the ball in the right center of the net as the keeper dives the other way.

Up by two goals now, we should be in good shape, even if we are still not reminding anybody of FC Barcelona with our creative playmaking. While Colombia's midfielder, Yoreli Rincon, my friend and former teammate, shows brief flourishes of great skill, as do her teammates, we continue to lurch impatiently around the box, showing little ability to break down the defense with any consistency.

Even when Colombia has to play a man down after the red card, we are not able to generate a whole lot. Whether it's bad passes or poor decision-making, our possession game isn't sharp, and that makes us dependent on a great individual play to create something. Kling delivers just that to set up my PK, slipping a sweet ball over to start Pinoe on her run. About ten minutes later, it's my turn to try to make a play. I get the ball in the attacking third, take a couple of people on, then hit a curling, right-footed shot toward the right side of the goal. The Colombian keeper dives to her left and smothers it.

I thought it had a chance and am bummed it didn't go in, but that's okay.

This is more like it, I think. *I'm starting to feel like myself.*

I can't tell you for sure, but I don't think I'd have made that run if I hadn't scored on the PK. The goal doesn't just put me on the board literally; it helps set me free psychologically. I'm nowhere near where I want to be, but I am getting closer.

As I head out of Commonwealth Stadium and board the bus for our hotel, there is finally a glimmer of a break in the storm clouds that have been hanging low and dark over my psyche for the whole World Cup.

It's happening slowly, but it's happening.

I am about to be unleashed, I think. *That PK is going to recharge me, uplift me. I am going to be a whole different player. You wait and see.*

I am named Player of the Match by the people on the FIFA Technical Committee. We're in the quarterfinals. I don't say it out loud to anyone, but as I look out the bus window at the big western Canadian sky, there's a single thought in my head, above all others:

I am back.

17

Addition by Subtraction

THE GOOD FEELING over our advancement into the final eight of the World Cup is tempered by the loss of two frontline players, Megan Rapinoe and Lauren Holiday. Both of them will miss our quarter-final against China in Ottawa for exactly what Jill and her staff were worried about with me: yellow cards. Pinoe and Lauren got carded for a second time in the Colombia game, and even though I think both of the calls were borderline at best, rules are rules. So now we go into our biggest game of the tournament without two mainstays.

Two nights before the China game, Jill asks me to visit her in her room.

"I'm thinking of changing things up and moving you forward and giving you room to roam behind the forward line," she says. "We can have Morgan [Brian] sitting behind you. I'm not set on this yet, but I think it's a good way to go. China is very organized defensively, and I think we're going to need for you to be more of a presence in the attacking third."

Not that I am taking credit for shifting Jill's thinking, but what she is suggesting is essentially what I tell the press after the Colombia game: that we need to open it up, play more freely, and exert high pressure on our opponents, coming after them from the start.

Jill shows me clips of the Chinese defense, and we talk some more about my expanded role. I'm so happy I could hug her. I want nothing more than to be a true attacking midfielder. For all the heat we've taken in this tournament — and the media is burying us, even after three victories and a tie — I know we have better soccer in us, and I think we're all ready to show it.

As if to prove it, I settle a ball in the second minute, see Amy Rodriguez making a run toward goal, and flick it ahead to her between two defenders. Amy is in alone, a quality chance right out of the chute, but with the keeper rushing at her, she shanks her shot wide.

Still, we send an early message to the Chinese, and we don't let up. We apply high pressure, and we keep possession when we win the ball. It doesn't result in immediate goals, but there's no question we are dominating play, particularly at the end of the half when we string together nine or ten straight passes, starting with Becky Sauerbrunn and Julie Johnston in the back. We have the ball zipping around like a pinball, and a quick combination from Ali Krieger to Alex to ARod leads to a corner kick. Anyone who is paying attention can see we are a different team, bringing an attack that wasn't there in the first four games.

The first half finishes scoreless, but I like what we are doing and know we are going to keep the pressure on. Kelley O'Hara and I combine for a good chance in the opening minutes of the second, and soon after, Tobin Heath fights hard for a fifty-fifty ball near midfield and draws a foul in the process. Kling quickly takes the free kick, sliding it over to Julie, who is completely unmarked. Julie lifts a long ball into the box. I see it coming and make a run toward the goal. Though I am tightly marked, I believe if I anticipate correctly I can get my head on the ball.

Julie's ball is perfect. I get a good read on it and jump up, heading the ball downward, knocking it past the Chinese goalkeeper. It takes until the fifty-first minute, but we are on the board. I run off to the corner to celebrate with a karate kick to the flag.

Two goals in two World Cup games? I will take it.

China doesn't seriously threaten for the rest of the second half, and for the first time in four games we are connecting and creating, scoring a victory that is much more one-sided than the 1–0 score line would suggest. For the second consecutive game, I am named Player of the Match. We move on to the semis to play Germany, which outlasted France in penalty kicks. Not many people give us much of a chance against Germany, two-time World Cup champions and the top-ranked team in the world, a side that has scored twenty goals and allowed only three in the tournament. (That's an impressive goal differential, even factoring in that the Germans scored ten of those goals in one game against Ivory Coast.) We're not concerned about who thinks what. We're concerned only with getting better.

Almost from the start of our training together a dozen years ago, James would be in my ear constantly, with that thick Aussie accent of his.

"Don't let the coach take you off the field," he would say. "Play so it is not even an option. You want to get beyond politics and drama and all the nonsense? Just be better than everybody else. Give them no choice but to play you."

Now he is saying pretty much the same thing. When I tell him that Jill wants to keep me in the more forward position, even with Pinoe and Holiday back from their suspensions, he says, "Great. You know what the deal is. Play so she won't even consider moving you back to where you were."

So that is my goal as we travel to Montreal for the semis. The difference in my mentality from where it was after the first three games is as far as Montreal is from Vancouver — the site of the World Cup final.

Once the Germans get by France, they are the popular pick to win the whole thing. Celia Sasic, their star striker, is the leading scorer in the tournament, with six goals. Her teammate Anja Mittag is right behind her with five. Their captain, Nadine Angerer, might be the best keeper in the world who is not named Hope Solo, and she proves it almost from the start, because after we absorb a few minutes of high-flying German pressure, we are in serious attack mode.

In the seventh minute, Julie runs onto a Pinoe corner kick, delivering a wicked header that Angerer makes a superb save on with her left foot. In the fourteenth minute, I slide a ball back to Tobin Heath, who threads it on the ground up the middle, a spectacular through ball that Alex runs onto. Alex one-times it, but again Angerer makes the stop with a left-footed block. Already this game feels as if it's a heavyweight battle. The pace is furious, the intensity as real as the grass is phony. It is the best we've played in the entire tournament by far. We're combining well, moving the ball quickly, making clever runs. The Germans look as if they have no idea how to handle us.

The half ends with no score, but we keep coming at them. We know Germany played 120 minutes against France, and we are the fresher team. I have a good chance on a header off of another Pinoe corner kicker in the opening minutes of the second half but don't get it on frame. Then, in the fifty-sixth minute, I chip a ball to Alex, and it looks as if it might be a breakaway before she gets tangled up with a defender and is called for a foul.

Germany has raised its level early in this half, and it is generating some threats. We just need to weather it and come back even stronger. In the fifty-ninth minute, Germany plays a seemingly harmless ball out of midfield that bounces toward our goal. Julie is in full retreat to clear it, but Germany's Alexandra Popp is running hard at goal and slips in front of Julie inside the box and is about to get off a shot from point-blank range when Julie, in desperation, reaches for Popp's left shoulder and hauls her to the ground. The whistle blows. The referee points to the spot and gives Julie a yellow card. She actually gets off light, because it easily could've been a red card for impeding the progress of a player going in on goal.

Julie has had a spectacular World Cup, but in this moment she is devastated by the opportunity she has given Germany to possibly steal the game. She starts to cry. Several players go over and put an arm around Julie to console her.

As Sasic steps forward to take the kick, Hope grabs her water bottle and goes for a stroll along the goal line. It is a very leisurely stroll. If there were flowers nearby, she would've stopped to pick them. She is out of the goal so long she could've gotten a card herself. Hope is clearly aiming to get in Sasic's head, to freeze her. At first Sasic looks as if she isn't sure she wants to take the kick. She seems to ask a few of her teammates if they want it. Hope finally returns to goal. Sasic puts her hands on her hips, looking very cavalier about the whole thing, then turns and claps her hands a few times. An instant before she starts her run-up she turns her head to the side and smiles. Now she makes her approach and drives a low, hard ball to the left. Hope dives to the right.

Celia Sasic's ball veers just outside the left post.

The game is still tied. The crowd of some 51,000 people in Olympic Stadium lets out a collective roar. I let out my own roar.

Sometimes, even in the heat of a big game, you can feel the momentum shift on the spot. This is one of those times.

There is no way we are losing this game, I tell myself.

I turn to Julie.

"Keep your head up. Don't worry about it," I tell her. A couple of others make the same point.

A few minutes later, I can see that Julie is still moping, beating herself up. I've gotten to know her well because she trained with James and me leading up to the World Cup. It's time to take a sterner approach.

"Cut that shit out, JJ. We have a game to win," I say.

About seven minutes after Sasic hits her ball wide left, I win control of a bouncing fifty-fifty ball and play it to Kling, who knocks it straight ahead to Alex, who has some space and is taking it. She's carrying the dribble near the top of the box when German defender Annike Krahn gets in her path and basically hip-checks her, sending Alex flying. Alex lands hard, and by the time she does, there is a whistle, a yellow card, and a penalty kick for the United States.

It is mine to take. It's not clear at all if Krahn's contact with Alex is inside or outside the box. For sure, the initial bump is outside. I am not going to explore the matter with the ref. I walk straightaway to get the ball and put it on the spot. I have already visualized the PK the night before. I am going to go exactly where I went against Colombia. I step back from the ball and go to my shooting position. I am leaning forward, slightly bent at the waist, eyes fixed on the ball,

nothing else. I don't look at the keeper or the crowd or anything else.
Just the ball. I start my approach with a series of baby steps and then
plant and kick, a clean, hard strike toward the upper right ninety. Angerer dives the opposite way. The ball rips into the net.

U.S. 1, Germany 0.

I take off running, clenching my fists, until my teammates catch
up and mob me. I kiss my left ring finger and point to the televi-
sion camera, my shout-out to Brian. Then it's back to business. There
are twenty-one minutes plus stoppage time remaining. There's lots of
work yet to do.

I want no part of bunkering and letting Germany seize control of
the game while we sit on our one-goal lead. I want to keep playing
the way we have the whole game. In the seventy-sixth minute, I spin
away from traffic, take a dribble, and nudge a ball out wide toward
Kelley O'Hara, who has just come on for Tobin and is making a run
down the right flank. It looks as if she might spring free before a German defender slide-tackles the threat away.

Kelley and I are not done, though. In the eighty-fourth minute,
Holiday steps in and strips a German player near midfield and makes
a run before knocking it out wide to the left, where Abby catches up
and settles it, playing it back to Kling. Kling edges into the middle,
takes two dribbles as I move away from her, and slips into an open
space in the left side of the box. Kling carves a great pass to me, and
I take four quick dribbles, beat the defender out wide, and then cut
a left-footed cross toward the middle, but away from Angerer. Kelley sees this all developing and makes a perfectly timed run, running
onto my cross and spearing it with her right foot — into the goal.

It's her first international goal, and her timing is impeccable.

U.S. 2, Germany 0.

Still, there can't be any letup. If Germany were to somehow answer quickly and make it a one-goal game, who knows what could
happen? It's the final minutes of the sixth game of the World Cup,
and I am going strong, powering up. I have James and Laurel Acres
and years of fitness work to thank for that. In the ninetieth minute,
the Germans are advancing the ball up the right side, and I make a

thirty-yard sprint to apply pressure and disrupt it. Honestly, it's probably not a sprint I would have made in the first couple of games when I was weighted down with discouragement. It's a sprint powered by belief. My energy supply feels inexhaustible. I go all out until the referee blows the whistle three times and points to midfield, and our whole bench rushes onto the field.

I am named Player of the Match for the third straight time, but the heroes are everywhere. Our back five completely shuts down the most explosive offense at this tournament, and Kling, especially, is huge on her overlapping runs. Morgan Brian, at twenty-two the youngest player on the team, suffered what looked to be a nasty head injury in a violent first-half collision in the air with Alexandra Popp but is almost perfect otherwise, keeping possession and playing with tremendous poise at holding mid. Hope totally gets into Sasic's head on the PK and makes the saves she needs to.

We are bound for Vancouver, British Columbia, and the World Cup final, a place few thought we would be even a week ago. I call James in Greece after the game.

"You're not done yet, Ms. Lloyd," he says. "You've trained for this moment for your whole life. This is no time to let up. Finish the job. Bring home the World Cup. Show the whole world the kind of player you are."

18

World-Beater

YOU KNOW HOW JAMES WOULD ALWAYS TELL ME, "Play every game as if it's a World Cup final"? He doesn't have to say a thing on July 5, 2015, because I am in BC Place in Vancouver, and it *is* a World Cup final. The stadium is on the north side of False Creek, an inlet that separates downtown from the rest of the city, and it is inundated with true USA soccer fans who are hoping to see the first happy ending to a World Cup since 1999.

I have my own room for the final, on the twenty-fourth floor of the Sheraton Vancouver Wall Centre, and everything is great the night before except that I keep waking up. I am thinking about the game, dreaming about the game. I don't visualize scoring five goals in the final, the way I did a few months earlier during a training session on Ark Road, but the game is in my head nonstop. I am so ready to play that my heart is racing, and I don't know how I am going to make it until the 5:00 PM kickoff. We have three team meals before the game, and each time we gather all I can think is, *Can't we just play already?*

I have so much energy I don't know what to do with it. After breakfast I go for my fifteen-minute jog through downtown. Some people recognize me and wave and wish me good luck. I smile and wave back and keep going. I feel as though I could run for days. I organize everything in my room into tidy piles — the keepsakes and the Player of the Match frames and the clothes I bought on the James-ordered shopping trip. I am the same neat freak on the day of a World Cup final as I was as a schoolgirl back on Black Baron Drive.

One of our massage therapists stretches me out, and after a bite of lunch I hydrate and stretch some more and relax in the room with my headphones on. I've done most of my visualization the night before, but I get some more done throughout the day, not focusing on results so much as the process of playing the game . . . tackling hard, sending passes near and far, being strong in the attacking third.

Finally, it is almost time to leave for the game. I look down from my window and see a big crowd of fans lining the barricaded walkway we'll take to get on our bus. There are hundreds of them, waiting to give us a proper send-off. We meet in the lobby and then walk through a gauntlet of rousing cheers and waving flags and choruses of the "I believe that we will win" chant that has swept through our fan base. I am filming it on my phone, smiling as I go. It is a very cool spectacle. I board the bus and go to my spot, second row from the back on the right. Once again it's time to cue up "Dreamer" on my iPod and reread James's final World Cup email.

Here's what he writes:

Ms. Lloyd,

I have spent a lot of time reflecting and the thing that sticks out the most to me is that you are once again going into this final as the best Carli Lloyd there ever was.

You have broken barriers again and gone to a level that no one was expecting and are on the brink of shocking the world again.

Today you will rise again because:

1) Apart from being the best Carli Lloyd ever, you are going into this game loaded with a mental state that no one else is carrying and the only player with a body that can carry an entire team.

2) Because you are going into this game knowing you haven't achieved anything yet and you will once again fight like an underdog that never gives up and claws her way to the top.

3) Because tactically you are playing in a position that allows you to express yourself and get into positions to win the game all on your own.

4) Because the Japanese rely on shapes rather than pressure and this will allow you to showcase the marvelous skill you possess and stick a dagger into the folks that dared to call you unskilled.

5) Because you are the only player that can take a game and own it.

6) Because you are the most intimidating and feared player on the planet and the Japanese know it.

Time to make this yours. Time to show the world that there is only one Ms. Lloyd.

As usual start simple and build. Play your game and act like the midfielder that you are. Combine, dribble, shoot, get on the end of crosses and get back and admirably help out on defense. A fighting and involved Carli Lloyd will get to the Japanese. You will make them fold and take over.

There will be no denying you if the underdog shows up again and owns this game. Go make this yours. You deserve it.

Signed
The Planner.

Reading over it again, I am filled with fresh gratitude for what my mentor/friend/trainer has done for me. James believed in me long before I did.

How do you thank somebody for that?

Jill sticks with the same lineup as the Germany game. I will be wearing the captain's armband again, along with my usual Nike Mercurial Vapor Super Fly boots, with the words FIVE PILLARS — the motto of the University Soccer Academy — written on the side of each. When we go over set plays beforehand, Jill says that the first corner will be one that has been designed for me. Assistant Tony Gustavsson is in charge of the set pieces, and he is the architect of it. We practiced it only one time, but it cleverly creates a formation that spreads the Japanese defense out. I think it has a real chance to work.

Jill huddles us up before we take the BC Place field. One of her best qualities as a coach is how straightforward she is. We're grown women, and we know what's in front of us. Jill honors that. She says simply, "We started this journey to get to this very point. You know what you need to do. There isn't much else to say. We are ready. Let's bring this trophy back home. Go out there, have fun, and enjoy it."

An explosion of noise greets us when we take the field, more than 50,000 people rocking the place. The sky is a smoky gray, and I mean literally smoky: wildfires are burning in the mountains outside the city, and by later that night it will get so bad that there will be an environmental alert.

I take my spot along the center circle, at the half-field line, in the shaded half of the pitch. Seconds away now. Adrenaline is coursing through my body at Daytona 500 speed.

Japan, the defending champion, kicks off, but Lauren Holiday wins possession of a bouncing ball almost immediately and chips it out wide to me. I get my first touch eleven seconds into the game. I take three dribbles, make a cut, and play it up to Alex, who knocks it out wide to Ali Krieger, who hits Tobin Heath, who centers it back to Alex. Alex's left-footed touch carries the ball a bit too far, but we connect five passes and are attacking not even thirty seconds into the game. I love it. We keep the combinations coming.

On our next foray into the Japanese end, Pinoe gets a pass from Kling and sends it crossfield to Morgan Brian. Morgan plays it to Ali and makes a run. Ali slips for a second but scrambles to her feet and finds her. Morgan carries the ball toward the goal line and lets fly with a cross that is blocked, drawing a corner kick.

It is the third minute. Pinoe lines up to take the corner. Tony's design has a cluster of players in front, hoping for a head ball to play, and several others spread around the box. I am about thirty yards out, seemingly a complete bystander. As Pinoe begins her approach to take the kick, I sprint into the box on a bit of a diagonal run. Pinoe's kick is well struck and rolls quickly into the box, untouched. The play is built 100 percent on timing. If the kick is too slow, or too fast, if I am too early or too late, it will go for nothing. Pinoe's corner is perfect. I run onto it and intersect with it just a stride inside the penalty spot. My focus is entirely on the ball, nothing else. I make contact with it with the outside of my left foot, and at the ball's pace and my pace, I do not have to strike it hard. The ball fires off my foot, a spinning rocket toward the left side of the Japanese goal. Keeper Ayumi Kaihori dives but has no chance. The ball blasts into the net, and after a momentary fall I bound right back up and keep on running, heading to the corner, fists pumping and celebrating in front of the American Outlaws and then hugging Pinoe and everybody else near the corner flag.

You could not ask for a better way to start.

It is not just one of our best goals of the whole tournament, but one of the best goals of the year — not because I score it but because the execution on everybody's part, especially Pinoe's corner and the player movements that opened up the space, is exactly as Tony drew it up. On the bench, Jill smiles and pats Tony on the left leg. The Japanese players look as if they've just been hit by a tractor-trailer.

The tractor-trailer is not stopping.

Tobin makes a great run down the right side and gets taken down just outside the box, and we have another set piece in the fifth minute. Holiday takes this one and drives it low and hard to Julie Johnston, who has edged toward the near post. I am at the 18-yard line and make a run as soon as Lauren makes contact. Julie's job is to get a piece of the ball and send it on behind her, into the middle, and she does it beautifully. The ball caroms toward the front of the goal, glances off a Japanese player's hand, and here I come, unmarked at first, crashing the goal, then beating two defenders to the ball and side-footing it past Kaihori to make it 2–0. BC Place is quaking it is so loud, and again I just keep on running, putting my arm around Lauren and then leading our whole team on a sprint across the field, all the way to the bench, where we have a spontaneous group hug.

Who can even believe this is happening? It is the greatest start to a World Cup game the U.S. has ever had, the greatest start to a game that I have ever had.

It is almost an out-of-body experience, the way this game has begun. Japan tries to settle itself and create the possession it is so good at, but Becky Sauerbrunn, a rock in the back the whole World Cup, intercepts a pass and plays it up to Morgan Brian, who directs it out wide to Tobin. Tobin takes a few touches and chips a long ball into the box, toward Alex, but a missed clearance leaves the ball bouncing inside the box, and Holiday takes full advantage, stepping up and volleying it, a superb strike that blows right past Kaihori, who must have no idea what has hit her.

We are in the fourteenth minute and we are up 3–0, and the rollicking fans are just cheering nonstop because they have no idea what else to do. The Japanese huddle up before the kickoff, trying somehow to stay composed and probably remind themselves that they have more than seventy-five minutes to get this level. It doesn't help. They connect ten passes on their next possession, but near the halffield circle I intercept a bad backpass and take a touch, eluding a Japanese player and starting upfield. I take a second touch and look up to see who is open and how best to attack, when I notice that Kaihori is off her line — way off her line — near the 18. I know if I hit it right I can get the ball over her and put it on goal.

I have been practicing these midfield shots with James for thirteen years.

It's worth a shot, I tell myself.

Maybe a foot inside the center line, fifty-four yards from the Japanese goal, I push the ball far enough in front of me that I can take a full swing at it. I power up to the ball and drive it toward the goal. Kaihori sees what I am doing and begins a desperate retreat. My ball has just the right trajectory, high enough to carry but low enough that Kaihori doesn't have much time to recover. She keeps retreating, and it doesn't make it any easier that I am shooting from the shadows and she is looking straight into the sun. She stumbles backwards at about the 6-yard line, and as she falls she manages to get her right hand on the ball, slightly redirecting it.

It is not enough.

The ball bounces once, ticks off the left post and into the net, with Ayumi Kaihori sprawled on her back right in front of it.

We have entered the realm of the surreal. Japan gave up two goals in the run of play in six previous games. And now we have scored four in sixteen minutes. Are you kidding? I am running and laughing, holding two index fingers aloft, trying to comprehend what is happening but knowing there is no chance. Hope almost never comes out of goal to celebrate, but she runs up to join us this time.

She hugs me and says, "Are you even human?"

I don't know what I am. I just know we are up 4–0 on a great team, sixteen minutes into the World Cup final, and we aren't letting up. It's barely two minutes later when Pinoe chips a sweet ball to Kling, who arches a perfect little cross in front. I go up and put a head on it, knocking it toward the near post, but just wide.

It might be the easiest chance I have had all day.

The Japanese break through in the twenty-seventh minute on a goal by forward Yuki Ogimi, who spins in the box and curls a beautiful shot into the upper left corner. They pick up their level at the end of the half, and Jill warns us at the break not to get complacent, not to sit back. We need to keep up the pressure and the attacking mentality that got us the lead.

Just five minutes into the second half, Japanese midfielder Aya Miyama takes a long free kick, which skims off Julie's head into the corner of the goal. Japan has cut our lead in half, and if we learned anything in the Cup final four years earlier, when Japan twice came back from one-goal deficits, this is not a team that goes away.

You can tell the Japanese are starting to believe they can do this, and there's still almost forty minutes to play. We need to answer. On our ensuing possession, we put pressure on the Japanese back line. I control a loose ball near the top of the box and carry it in and push it ahead to Alex. She is rebuffed, but we keep possession, and soon Kling and Alex work a nice give-and-go that leads to a corner kick. Holiday lofts it right in front of the goal. Kaihori tries to punch it away but muffs the clearance, and the ball goes beyond her to Morgan Brian, who centers it to Tobin, who is unmarked in front and pounds it in.

The lead is back to three, and we are not letting up. I win a ball in the middle third and make my longest run of the day deep into the attacking third before hitting Pinoe on the left side of the box. I nearly take advantage of sloppy Japanese defense and almost beat Kaihori to a backpass before she grabs it. Kelley O'Hara, who comes on for Pinoe, continues her dynamic play and has two good chances right away.

The game moves beyond the seventieth minute, and Japan is playing some of its best soccer of the game. Hope makes a fine clearance on a high ball, and the defense stays tight and organized, giving the supremely skilled Japanese little room to create.

In the seventy-ninth minute, the greatest goal-scorer in the history of international soccer, Abby Wambach, comes on for Tobin. A huge ovation resounds through BC Place. I go over to the sideline, take off the captain's armband, and strap it on Abby. This will be the final World Cup game of her career. It's only right that she goes out with the armband.

The clock keeps moving, but I am oblivious to it. Even as I see our bench and coaching staff standing arm-in-arm, I am fighting for loose balls, trying to keep possession. Now we move into extra time, one minute and then another and then a third, and I am chasing a ball that sails over my head when the three whistles blow and the stadium erupts one more time.

I drop to my knees and am almost instantly overcome by emotion. I don't cry in public, ever. I guess I make an exception when we win a World Cup. The coaches and the whole team pour onto the field, running so fast you'd think they were being chased. Heather O'Reilly is the first to reach me. She bends down and wraps her arms around me, and there we are in BC Place by False Creek, two Jersey girls reveling in the happy, smoky moment. Other players head to the edge of the field to find their family and friends and drink in the love. I don't go over to the stands, because I don't think anybody is there. Soon enough, I find out I am wrong; Aunt Patti, my cousins Jaime and Adam, and my best friend Karen have all secretly made the trip for the final. Brian thought hard about it but in the end wanted to respect my wishes.

My parents? They are not here. I don't even know if they watched. I never hear a word until my mother sends a card a few weeks later.

After the medal ceremony, and after I receive the Golden Ball for being the Player of the Tournament, I return to the locker room and can't find my phone at first, because it's somewhere beneath all the layers of cellophane they've covered the locker room with to protect our stuff from spraying champagne. When I finally dig it out, there are more than 400 text messages. I call Brian first, and it's so wonderful to hear the joy in his voice.

"I am so happy and proud of you," Brian says.

"I can't wait to celebrate with you," I say.

When I reach James, he says, "What's going on?"

"Not much," I say. "Just won a World Cup and scored some goals."

"I told you you could do it," he says.

"I know. And I am not stopping now. When are we training next? I want to keep getting better."

James stops me. "Ms. Lloyd, relax and enjoy the moment. We will train soon enough."

I meet up with Aunt Patti, Jaime, Adam, and Karen.

I hug them all and tell them, "I can't believe you are here!" Jaime and Karen stay with me in my room that night, even though I never go to bed. I am way too wired and way too happy to sleep. The team party goes loud and late. For once I am not in my room, hydrating and stretching. I am in the middle of everything. It's the best sleepless night of my life.

19

Pure Gold

ONE HUNDRED NINETY-ONE DAYS after our triumph over Japan and what people are calling the greatest performance in the history of the World Cup finals, I have traded in my white number 10 USA uniform and Nike boots for a red Matthew Christopher gown and high heels. I am with Brian, sitting directly behind Ronaldo in the second row of a huge auditorium in a swanky building called Kongresshaus, on the shores of Lake Zurich in Switzerland.

The event is FIFA's annual gala, Ballon d'Or (French for "Gold Ball"). The date is January 11, 2016. I have played soccer all over the world, but I've never been to Zurich until now. I am here because I am a finalist for the most prestigious award a soccer player can receive — FIFA's World Player of the Year. The greatest players in the sport are all around me, among them Lionel Messi, Neymar, and my personal favorite, Andres Iniesta, the incomparable midfielder for FC Barcelona. On the women's side, the notables include my fellow finalists, Aya Miyama of Japan and Celia Sasic of Germany, the star players of our last two opponents in the World Cup, along with my friend and teammate, Hope Solo, who was on the short list for Player of the Year honors, as well.

I am accompanied by my three allotted guests: Brian, James, and James's oldest son, Astin. The room is very warm, and between that and my nerves — I am more nervous by far than I've ever been for an Olympic or World Cup final — my hands and feet are slick with sweat. I've been nervous ever since I arrived in Switzerland, almost unable to eat, sleeping fitfully, my fuel mostly consisting of cappuccinos. Brian and I are holding hands, but I keep having to pull away to dry myself off a bit. When you play you can work out the nerves by running for a ball or tackling somebody. At Ballon d'Or there is nothing to do but sit and wait and hope your name is called, kind of like FIFA's version of the Oscars.

Between the time the master of ceremonies says, "I proudly present the FIFA Women's World Player of the Year," and opens the envelope, it feels as if a full ninety minutes goes by, plus ten minutes of stoppage time. I think my heart might pound right out of my gown. It keeps pounding until I hear the emcee say:

Carli Lloyd.

I want to get up and run around as if I were celebrating a goal, but I play it cool instead. The happiness I feel is almost indescribable. I give Brian a kiss and begin the walk up onto the stage, careful to lift up the gown so as not to trip, pausing to shimmy my foot back on the heel because it has slipped out from the sweat. I successfully make it up the steps without a tumble and gratefully receive the trophy, which is so heavy I could do curls with it.

"Wow," I say.

I am overcome in the moment and take four or five seconds to collect myself. I apologize, and the crowd applauds. Finally, I think I'm calm enough to get through my remarks, which I've been thinking about for a couple of days.

Here's what I say:

"It truly is an honor. This has been a dream of mine ever since I started my journey with the national team.

"Celia . . . Aya . . . [You are] phenomenal footballers just as deserving of this award.

"I want to thank everyone who voted for me. Also I want to thank Sunil Gulati and everyone at U.S. Soccer for all their support. I also want to thank Jill [Ellis] and the coaching staff [and] all of our support staff. I honestly wouldn't be sitting up here — standing up here — without my incredible teammates, and we all know it took twenty-three players to win the World Cup this past summer, so thank you to them.

"To my friends and family at home, thank you for your support. To my fiancé Brian, I couldn't have done this without your support. I love you. To James, we started this journey thirteen years ago. You told me that I could become the best player in the world. It just took me the realization now that I could. Thank you for everything. One last shout-out: Astin Galanis, Preston Galanis, keep working hard. Keep your dream and just go after 'em.

"Thank you, everybody."

The whole night is a blur. It gets even better when Jill Ellis, who took over our team just over a year out from the World Cup, is named the Women's Coach of the Year. Afterwards, I pose for photos with Messi, the men's Ballon d'Or winner, and get to meet Ronaldo, Marcelo, Kaka, and a who's who of other world-class players. I even sneak in a quick photo with Iniesta.

The gala dinner is in the room next door, but even then I barely eat because I am too excited and people keep coming by and wanting photos. It is a blast, but by now I really want out of the gown and heels. Brian and I go back to the hotel to change; the only clothes I have are my U.S. training pants and a long-sleeved T-shirt, so that's what I go with. We head down to the hotel bar, where we meet up with Jill and our FIFA liaisons. For me that is Rebecca Smith, a former national team player for New Zealand, who is my guide the whole time in Zurich. She is awesome and wants to make sure everything goes perfectly. Rebecca orders me a shot of tequila, the only drink I have the whole night.

Not much of a party girl. No reason to start now.

I order a cheeseburger and fries — a meal I have maybe once a year—and Brian and I are just relaxing and hanging out. We don't stay up late because Brian has an early flight back to the States. I fly a bit later on with Jill, Hope, and Hope's husband Jerramy. Reclining in a business-class seat/bed, I watch the film *San Andreas* and catch up on sleep and try to comprehend everything that has happened in the last twenty-four hours, my mind wandering at 40,000 feet, a barrage of disjointed thoughts and feelings coming at me from everywhere.

Did this all really just happen? Am I really returning home from the Ballon d'Or? Did I really hear my name called out before the greatest players in the world, after being voted FIFA's Women's World Player of the Year?

When you work toward a goal for this long, you can't even fathom how you might feel once you achieve it. I still cannot fathom it now, and in some ways I am not sure I even want to, because I do not want to stop here. I want to keep getting better and better. I don't want to be satisfied, ever. That may sound grim, but it isn't at all. It is joyful, because the pursuit of progress is joyful. Playing the game I love is joyful.

So I keep pushing, keep working.

I am, after all, a soccer player. Not a brand. Not a celebrity. Why complicate things with image-making or pretension? Give me a ball and let's go. That is how true soccer players are.

"When you are on the field, you aren't competing against anybody," James says. "You are competing against yourself. The competition is who you were yesterday and your goal is to be better than that today. Your opponent on match day is not another team; it's your previous performance."

Not every performance will be better than the one before, of course. The first three games of the World Cup were a painful reminder of that. The point is that if you are not driven to improve, the only possible options are staying the same or getting worse, neither of which is acceptable.

It seems like decades ago now, but at one time I wanted to quit soccer. My U-21 coach, Chris Petrucelli, sent me packing from the national team, telling me that I wasn't good enough and didn't work hard enough. For a time I was ready to accept his assessment and go find a job that didn't involve cleats and shin guards, but then my father connected me with a man named James Galanis and everything changed.

James offered me so much more than deep soccer expertise. He offered me hope. He offered belief. He offered a commitment of time and energy that was beyond all measure — truly 24/7, 365 days a year — and for no charge, because he saw the possibilities.

In so many words, James told me this:

You have skills and an understanding of the game that are hard to teach. But you also are mentally weak, quick to blame others, inclined to be lazy, and terribly unfit. It will take a lot of work — years of work — but if you want it, I believe you can be not only a fixture on the U.S. Women's National Team. I believe you can be the best player in the world.

If that is indeed what you want, let's get to work.

It seems the realm of pure fantasy, doesn't it? A little-known trainer from South Jersey is going to take on a U-21 reject and make her the world's best player? Right. And for his next trick, he will swim to Australia and back.

More than a few people thought James was completely grandiose or a charlatan, or both. They thought I was a misguided minion who had fallen under his spell. Nobody believed. Even James's wife Colleen had her doubts. What very few understood was how hard we worked, all year round, at all hours of the night and day. It would've been easy to cut corners, but we never did because we knew we couldn't, and that is how we are doing things even now.

So there we are under the dim-watt bulbs on Ark Road, working on side volleys in the cold and damp of December. There we are, refining first touches and crosses in the heat and humidity of July. There we are in the Blue Barn in winter, or in Laurel Acres whenever, James devising the workout plans and me punishing my body according to his specifications.

There are scores of world-class players, maybe hundreds of them, who are deeply committed to their work and who train incredibly hard. I would never say that I outwork all of them, because how could I really know that? All I can tell you is that for thirteen years James Galanis and I, mentor and pupil, have poured every ounce of our energy and passion into this mad-scientist project of his.

Whatever else you want to say, it's worked out pretty well.

James secretly loved that nobody believed in us, and he taught me to love it. He relished it when I was benched or criticized or overlooked, when other U.S. players were commanding the spotlight, because he knew it would be gasoline for my internal fire. What can I tell you?

I thrive on that Jersey edge.

I love to prove people wrong.

Now that my teammates and I are World Cup champions and I've been named FIFA's Women's Player of the Year, I'm not sure how I will continue to be an underdog. But trust me, I will find a way. Somebody will write that it was a fluke, or that I am over the hill, or that I just got really lucky in those opening sixteen minutes against Japan. Or maybe it will be something else. Whatever it is, I will find someone to prove wrong and then work my ass off to do just that.

I can't tell you that the path I've taken has been easy. It has been filled with doubts and despair, tears and trauma, with a difficult family situation that I still hope can be healed and overcome. I've said it before and will say it again: without my parents, none of this — the World Cup and Olympic titles, my career, to say nothing of this book — would've been possible.

I don't know all the answers, or even half of them. I just know what works for me. So what do I want to leave you with? Listen to your heart and try always to do the right thing. Put everything you have into your passions, because one of the greatest gifts in life is to be able to do what you love. Cherish the people who love and support you unconditionally, for they are life's greatest treasure.

Life is complicated. Life is going to throw all kinds of obstacles in your way. All I can tell you is what works for me: be true to yourself, don't do fake, and above all else, keep on working, because that's what will take you where you want to go.

Epilogue
Priorities, Progress, Passion

OUR SO-CALLED VICTORY TOUR following the 2015 World Cup wasn't even forty-five minutes old when I'd already started thinking about our next major competition — the 2016 Olympics in Brazil. It's just how I am wired. I won my first Olympic gold at age twenty-six, the second at age thirty, and my first World Cup title at thirty-three. I can rest later. Now I want to work. Now I want to get better. I want to hit the training field with James Galanis and defy the notion that athletic life after thirty is just a messy, inexorable tumble into mediocrity.

Nothing stokes me like a challenge, and that's what keeps me going. It's what has driven me from the very beginning of this journey, completely embracing James's words about turning my weaknesses into strengths. For all of us, in every profession and walk of life, it's easy to take on things that come naturally and present no challenge. Working on the things you are not so good at is infinitely harder. It takes courage to make an honest self-assessment and fix what needs fixing. One of the first realizations I had with James was that I am not naturally fit. I thought I was fit, but I was fooling myself. I've spent years working on that weakness, and now I truly believe it is one of my greatest strengths.

If my career has taught me anything, it's that nothing worthwhile in life comes easily. That's just the way it is, and the way it should be.

If it were easy, it wouldn't mean nearly as much when you achieve your goal.

The fact is that I never feel more alive, more energized, than when I am working toward a goal. I am as transparent as a pane of glass. I love it when people doubt me, because it's just another chance to prove them wrong. Crafting an image? Building a brand? I don't think so. As trite as it might sound, all I want to do is be a better person and better player today than I was yesterday, and better still tomorrow. I want to be a positive role model and empower young female athletes and inspire them to aim high and not let any obstacles sidetrack them. That's why our team filed a wage-discrimination complaint against U.S. Soccer late in 2015, an action taken to address the massive pay gap between the men and women who wear the Team USA jersey. That's why it was so important to write a completely honest book and not airbrush away adversity. Life is hard. Competitive sports is hard. The people who succeed don't heed the doubters and don't give in to despair or negativity. They don't talk about emptying the tank, they just empty it. It's just one more indispensable life lesson I've learned from my mentor, coach, and friend James Galanis, who even now never stops reminding me that you can achieve great things in life if you are true to yourself, and you do the work when nobody is watching.

Afterword

I'VE HAD A LOT of great days in my life. Days when I've scored goals to win Olympic gold medals. Days when I helped the United States win a World Cup and when I've been honored as FIFA's World Player of the Year. All were hugely thrilling in their own way, but my greatest day of all was November 4, 2016, when I married the love of my life, Brian Hollins.

Brian and I exchanged our vows at the edge of the Caribbean Sea on the Mayan Riviera of Mexico, surrounded by sun, sand, and eighty family members and friends. I ran on the beach in the morning, said "I do" on the beach in the afternoon, and then we all celebrated on the beach well into the night.

I love the water. I've been going to my aunt Patti and aunt Sandy's house on the Jersey Shore since I was a little kid. Brian and I always talked about a beach wedding somewhere warm, at a destination spot with a small group of the people we love the most.

It was perfect.

Soon enough we settled into our new life together, and I went back into the workshop with James, training in the Blue Barn. There was an upcoming U.S. Women's National Team camp to prepare for, as well as the 2017 NWSL season. Unbeknownst to me, I was also prepping for one of the greatest opportunities a footballer could ever ask for.

Brian and I had planned for some time to spend the Christmas holiday in England, along with James, his wife, Colleen, and their sons, Astin and Preston. We caught an Arsenal match in London and then went up to Liverpool to take in two matches, having been invited by the club after they found out I was a big fan. It was a trip out of a soccer dream, and then it got even better, with a side trip to Manchester, a city of a half-million people in northwest England and one of the most renowned soccer towns on earth.

Not long before we left the States, my management team received an email from Nick Cushing, manager of Manchester City's women's team, inquiring as to whether I might be interested in visiting the Man City facilities. Gavin Makel, head of women's football at the club, connected with James. The details were worked out. It was all very informal. No hard sell at all. I had gotten interest from some foreign clubs in the past, but nothing ever came of it. I figured we were over there and might as well take a look, so the whole pack of us — James and Colleen, Astin and Preston, Brian and I — toured the club's 80-acre facility.

There's only one word to describe my reaction:

Unbelievable.

The complex is practically a city unto itself, with sixteen-and-a-half fields and state-of-the-art everything, including gyms, meal rooms, hot and cold tubs, physio spaces, a team hotel, and even a boot-cleaning station. It's world-class all the way, and the club's commitment to building a women's team that is on par with its men's team is totally apparent. Taking it all in, I had the same feeling I had when I was a little girl and got my first pair of real soccer cleats. I just wanted to get out there and play.

The more I thought about it, the more the timing seemed perfect. It wasn't an Olympic year or a World Cup year. The commitment would only be for three-plus months — for the English Football Association's Super League season, along with the FA Cup and UEFA Champions League. We started to talk, but before I committed to anything, I knew that I had to clear it with Jill Ellis and Sunil Gulati, the president of U.S. Soccer, as well as the Houston Dash, my NWSL team. Jill encouraged me to go for it, and though the Dash was obviously disappointed I wouldn't be there at the start of the season, they agreed it was a great opportunity for me. Man City and I reached an agreement, and soon I was moving into a beautiful apartment in the same building as Pep Guardiola, manager of the Man City men's team, and some of the men's team's players. Better still, I scored on a header in my first Champions League game, set up on a beautiful cross from Jane Ross, and then added another goal in the semifinals. We wound up losing to Lyon, but we definitely announced ourselves as a club on the rise.

And that, for me, is what this is all about — playing at the highest possible level. I don't want to stay the same, ever. Let people talk about my age and how my body won't let me do what I used to do. All that does is motivate me. I want to keep raising the proverbial bar. From the time I started training with James, the goal was to get better every day. Nothing has changed. We have a World Cup title to defend in 2019. We have some Olympic amends to make in 2020, after our unhappy result in Brazil, where we lost to Sweden on PKs in the quarterfinals. There's always a new challenge ahead. It's one of my favorite things about life. You wake up and have a fresh opportunity to go beyond where you've ever gone before. What could be better than that?

> — Carli Lloyd
> *Mount Laurel, New Jersey*
> *June 2017*

Acknowledgments

I've known for a long time that it takes eleven players to make a strong soccer team. I've learned that it takes many more players than that to make for a successful book.

Josh Weil and Jay Mandel at William Morris Entertainment set this project in motion, connecting me with a top-notch publisher in Houghton Mifflin Harcourt and a wonderful editor in Susan Canavan. Susan believed in the project and its message from the outset, and so did the whole world-class team at HMH: Bruce Nichols, Jenny Xu, Martha Kennedy, Megan Wilson, Hannah Harlow, Rachael DeShano, and Cindy Buck.

I want to thank everyone at U.S. Soccer. The senior officials, coaches, medical staff, trainers, massage therapists, equipment managers, and support staff — all of you are consummate pros and have played a huge role in supporting and helping me throughout my career.

I am lucky to have the support of such great sponsors. Thank you for believing in me.

So many people in the Delran community have encouraged me from the time I started playing. I can't begin to name them all, but Delran is where my journey began and you were all a huge part of it.

Rudi Klobach, late coach of Delran High School, led our team to two state championship games and was as passionate about soccer as anyone I've ever met. All of my teammates at Delran High were a part of memories that will stay with me forever. The late Joe Dadura, founder and inspiration of the Medford Strikers, provided me with six of the best years of my soccer life and with friendships that have lasted even longer. To Kacy, Maureen, Venice, and Quinn — PITA will never forget you, or the Original 5. To all of my Strikers teammates, thank you for making every practice and every game so much fun.

My thanks to my Rutgers coach, Glenn Crooks, for giving the great gift of allowing me to play with freedom and creativity — to express myself on the field. I was fortunate to have such wonderful room-mates and teammates as Tara Froehlich and Christine Wentzler and so many other tremendous Scarlet Knight teammates over four years.

Jerry Smith gave me a chance with the U-21s, and I have never forgotten that. Chris Petrucelli gave me honesty that changed my life. Jill Ellis was a wonderful coach with the U-21s, and I have enjoyed continuing this journey with her; thank you for your respect and be-lief in me, Jill.

For years the people of Evesham Township, New Jersey, have gen-erously allowed me the use of the Blue Barn to train in. Without the Blue Barn, this story never would've happened.

The students and staff of Universal Soccer Academy have been my soccer soul mates forever. Thank you for helping me become a better player and human being.

There's nothing more special than friendship. Thanks to Heather Mitts, my longtime teammate and training buddy, who understood and befriended me from the start. You have always been there for me and helped me along the way. Thank you. Hope Solo is not only a world-class goalkeeper, she has been a dear friend to me on an un-forgettable journey. Thank you for always believing in me and being there for me.

John Johnson, my attorney, has always looked after me and pro-tected me. You have been such an important piece of my success, and I can't thank you enough. You are the best lawyer anyone could have. Karen and Kathy Sweet are twin sisters and twin best friends, and I cannot tell you how much I cherish you both for your amazing love and friendship.

To my soon-to-be in-laws, Kathy Hollins, Bob Hollins, Lisa, Jim, Tyler and Kyle Gonteski, Lucy Ebert, Debbie Teisman, Ann Marie and Amanda Holloway, Ed, Joe and Chris Ebert — thank you for all your kindness and support. Soon we will all officially be family.

To Colleen, Astin, and Preston Galanis, you have all become my extended family, and I can't thank you enough for all your support. I love you guys.

Jaime Bula, my cousin, was my idol growing up and is now my biggest supporter. Thank you for always being there for me.

Aunt Patti, Aunt Sandy, and Uncle Wayne — you have always been there for me, in good times and bad. The support you have provided me throughout my life has been priceless, and I can't thank you enough for being there for me. Uncle Phil — I miss you and will never forget the time you gave me a bloody nose. You toughened me up! You have always been my number-one fan — I know you are celebrating my journey from above. To my grandfather, Pop-pop, I miss you and my grandmom Carol, thank you for all our fun times and visits together. I will forever cherish those moments. To my cousins — Adam Wilson, Brent Carr, Kerrie DaVanon, Bryan and Craig Wilson — you are the best, and I hope you know that.

The Bula, DaVanon, Jackson, Carr, and Fornaro families have long been a major part of my life. I love you all.

To James's mom, Vicky, thanks so much for all of your support — all the way from Down Under.

My co-author Wayne Coffey showed amazing dedication throughout the writing process and pushed and prodded me to make the message of this book authentic and empowering. I cannot thank him enough for the countless hours he put in to tell my story.

Thank you to my parents for being there for me throughout my younger years as a soccer player. Your dedication and commitment to helping me follow my dreams is very much appreciated. I will never forget the times I shared with you both on the soccer field and at home. Without you, I would not be who I am today. To my sister Ashley and brother Stephen, I thank you for everything you have done for me. We had great times together growing up, and I will forever cherish these moments.

Brian Hollins is not just the man I am about to marry. He is my love, my everything. He is the most patient man on earth. I can't thank you enough for all the support you have given me throughout my journey. None of this would have been possible without your love and support. I cannot wait to be your wife. I love you more than anything, Brian.

James Galanis has so many roles in my life I am not sure where to start. He is a professor, a trainer, a mentor, a friend. He saved my career, believed in me when no one else did, set a goal, and never wavered from working hard each and every day to make it happen. It took me thirteen years to realize that I could become the best player in the world. He taught me how to become strong and conquer anything that comes my way.

I can try to thank you for all that you've done for me as a player and person, James, but words would never be enough. I guess they'll have to do, though, won't they, mate?

— Carli Lloyd

Photo Credits

Insert 1

Page 1: *(top)* Welsh Photography, John Welsh; *(bottom)* Courtesy of the author

Page 2: *(top)* Welsh Photography, John Welsh; *(bottom)* Courtesy of the author

Page 3: *(top)* Courtesy of the author; *(bottom)* Courtesy of the author

Page 4: *(top)* From *Courier-Post*, 2012-07-06, © 2016 Gannett-Community Publishing. All rights reserved. Used by permission and protected by the Copyright Laws of the United States. The printing, copying, redistribution, or retransmission of this content without express written permission is prohibited; *(bottom)* Courtesy of Rutgers University Division of Intercollegiate Athletics

Page 5: *(top)* Courtesy of FOX Sports; *(bottom)* © Brad Smith/isiphotos.com

Page 6: *(top)* © Leslie Benedict/isiphotos.com; *(bottom)* © Koji Watanabe/Getty Images

Page 7: *(top)* © Brad Smith/isiphotos.com; *(bottom)* Courtesy of the author

Page 8: *(top)* © M. Stahlschmidt/SSP; *(bottom)* © M. Stahlschmidt/SSP

Insert 2

Page 1: *(top)* © John Todd/isiphotos.com; *(center)* © M. Stahlschmidt/SSP; *(bottom left)* © John Todd/isiphotos.com; *(bottom right)* © M. Stahlschmidt/SSP

Page 2: *(top)* © M. Stahlschmidt/SSP; *(center)* © Tim Bouwer/isiphotos.com; *(bottom)* © John Todd/isiphotos.com

Page 3: *(top)* © Mike Hewitt/FIFA, Getty Images; *(center)* © M. Stahlschmidt/SSP; *(bottom)* © Dennis Grombkowski/ Getty Images

Page 4: *(top)* © M. Murray/SSP; *(bottom)* © Brad Smith/isiphotos.com

Page 5: *(top)* © L. Benedict/SSP; *(bottom left)* © Steven Limentani/ isiphotos.com; *(bottom right)* Courtesy of The YGS Group/*Philadelphia Inquirer.* Photo by Sarah J. Glover.

Page 6: *(top)* © Rob Kim/Getty Images; *(bottom)* © Kevin Mazur/Getty Images

Page 7: *(top)* © Jim Watson/Getty Images; *(bottom)* © Mike Hewitt/FIFA, Getty Images

Page 8: *(top)* Courtesy of NBC Universal Archives; *(bottom)* © Leigh Ann Ronczka

Index